HEY, HEY, JULIE!
N.R YES NO
maxell
POSITION: NORMAL
90
A

BASEMENT SONGS

A MEMOIR

ONE SONG AT A TIME IN A LIFETIME OF MUSIC

BY SCOTT MALCHUS

BasementSongsthebook.blogspot.com
Facebook.com/BasementSongsTheBook Twitter.com/MrMalchus

For information, address malcflynn@gmail.com

Malchus, Scott 1969-
Basement Songs / Scott Malchus

ISBN 978-0-578-11551-1

Cover artwork and design by Joseph Game
www.chogrin.com

The contents of this book first appeared in a slightly different form on Popdose.com.
The chapter "Landslide" is previously unpublished.

www.popdose.com

For Julie, Sophie and Jacob

CONTENTS

So long as the human spirit thrives on this planet, music in some living form will accompany and sustain it and give it expressive meaning.

Aaron Copland

FOREWORD

By Jeff Giles

There's an old maxim that says – stop me if you've heard this one before – that writing about music is like dancing about architecture. It's funny (you can't dance about architecture, ha ha), but it's also kind of true. It was especially true in the early days, when music writers tended to have things like degrees in "English" or "journalism" and fell back on all-but-dead concepts like objectivity and music theory in their work.

Those days are gone now, of course; with the advent of rock, the old guard no longer had the tools to sufficiently express the medium they were writing about, and by the time the rock press stumbled into the pop culture dawn, yawning and scratching their privates while venting their spleens all over some poor band's sophomore record, the entire discipline was broken open like an egg. Sure, there were still some fuddy-duddies in the bunch, but whether you were rocking along with Lester Bangs or studying at the loafer-encased foot of Christgau (the Dean of American Rock Critics, as he'd be happy to tell you), the writing still had a little more heat in it than before. A little more life.

And then you know what happened next: the Internet. All bets were off. Any asshole with a word processor could stand on a rock and call himself a publisher, and guys like Chuck Klosterman were proving that a writer could successfully wed compelling thinkspeak with navel-gazing B.S. on a regular basis. The guys who overturned the dust-covered tables in the halls of music criticism during the '60s were now the old guard, and much as their forebears had done decades previous, they regarded the rise of their successors with a gravely arched eyebrow and a disdainful snort. But it was too damn bad: The egg was broken all over again, this time along with the whole stupid entertainment industry. For the first time since the advent of mass media, everyone is a critic – and, probably more importantly, nobody needs one.

All of which is meant to explain, in a roundabout way, how a guy like Scott Malchus ended up writing the book you're holding. I've known Scott for some years now, and I'd be willing to bet you the price of a beer that he'd be uncomfortable calling himself a music critic – and in the not-so-distant past, his thoughts on the subject would have been confined to notebooks, Word documents, or B.S. sessions with his buddies.

Here's what I'm trying to say: Thank goodness for the Internet. What makes Scott a hesitant critic is what makes him so damn appealing as a writer. Unlike most of his peers in these irony-laden times, when to troll your wares on the Web you have to practice the emotional equivalent of wearing a lead-lined suit of armor whenever you wander near a comments section, Scott is unwilling or unable to pretend he's lost access to the childlike joy of experiencing great music. He doesn't analyze, he *feels*. And then he distills those feelings into honest, heartfelt prose. There's no wall between Scott and the reader. He writes with total disregard for prevailing trends and seemingly without thought for his own perceived coolness, which is admirable – and a lot harder than it looks when you're playing for an audience. The net result, as you're soon to see for yourself, is that you come away from his writing feeling like you've made a friend.

I've enjoyed being a member of Scott's audience – and privileged to call him friend – for quite a while now, and when I started Popdose, he was on my first wish list of contributors for the site. I knew people would respond to *Basement Songs* the same way I did – that they'd hear their own voice in Scott's, that they would feel his pain and joy bound up in these songs, the same way they did their own. Not to put too fine a point on it, but *Basement Songs* gets to the heart of why we listen to music in the first place: It helps us understand life a little better, sweetens our highs, underscores our lows. It's the echo of our shared experience, and Scott lets it ring true, unfettered by snark or pretenses to objectivity.

Writing about music, goes the old saying, is like dancing about architecture. But Scott Malchus dances the way we were born to

move: Gracefully, free of pretense, never taking a step for granted. His words will move you, too.

Jeff Giles is the founder and editor-in-chief of Popdose.com and Dadnabbit.com, as well as an entertainment writer whose work can be seen at Rotten Tomatoes and a number of other sites.

INTRODUCTION
"THE RAINBOW CONNECTION"

I grew up in North Olmsted, Ohio, a West Side suburb of Cleveland, where my parents owned a large four-level house. I have a brother, Budd, and two sisters, Beth and Heidi, and when we were kids the basement was essentially a dumping ground for toys. My dad's workbench occupied a space, essentially a dumping ground for his tools. When my brother, Budd, reached adolescence, he began playing the drums and decided to clean up the hole. In one corner he placed his black five-piece Rogers drum set. In the opposite corner, he laid down ugly green shag carpet he must have found on the side of the road and set up a cheap JCPenney stereo with four speakers mounted to the cinderblock walls. That half of the basement began to resemble a dorm room, with a couple of old couches and one of our grungy, yellow-upholstered reclining rockers creating a social atmosphere.

Soon posters of bands like Rush and Journey were hanging alongside the images of bikini clad babes hawking Budweiser and St.

Pauli Girl. How my parents can claim that they didn't know the basement was a haven for underage drinking is a mystery. Even though Budd used the basement as a rehearsal space for the numerous pickup bands he played in (or as a last resort beer binge hangout for his friends), my brother wasn't home much. He always had something to do or someplace to be. Gradually, I took up residence in the basement, and it became my Fortress of Solitude.

When I was 7 or 8, I took an interest in rock 'n roll. My parents had never been into rock music. My dad listened to classical, and my mom preferred show tunes or standards (what was then called elevator music), so my discovery of rock came independently, through the influence of friends, the tastes of the local deejays and from hanging with my brother. During those early years, Budd listened to Boston's debut album, Bob Seger's *Stranger in Town* and a copy of Eric Clapton's *Slowhand*, which somehow never made it back to its original owner after a band rehearsal. Besides these best-selling albums and the songs on the radio, there were also the three-chord, easy-to-learn tunes like "Rocky Mountain Way" and "25 or 6 to 4" that carried through the house during those pickup band rehearsals.

At the age of 11, I received a cassette recorder for Christmas. I'm not sure why it was given to me, but I used the thing to death, religiously placing it next to stereo speakers and taping songs directly off the radio. I guess you could say this was the beginning of the basement songs. I would collect tapes of my favorites and then head downstairs to listen in private, trying to decipher what the singers were saying and figure out what the drummers were playing – I, too, eventually became a drummer. A new world was opening up, and the basement became the one place where I could go to explore it.

I spent hours just *listening*, absorbing the music and appreciating the intricacies. I would occasionally study the album jacket, tracing my fingers over the artwork, some of it raised to give a 3-D effect. Music soon began to seep into every detail of my life: I tacked to my bedroom walls pictures torn out from magazines like *Circus* and *Hit Parader* and adorned the covers of my notebooks with the hand-drawn logos of the bands I worshipped. I treasure those early days of discovering music – and, more importantly, what those songs said to me emotionally and how they guided me through my life. As I grew older and the basement became a place to gather my thoughts and figure out life, the music became an accompaniment to the journey, not just background noise.

Ironically, what I consider my very first basement song isn't even a rock song. It's a pop song attributed to a green frog hand puppet: "The Rainbow Connection" from *The Muppet Movie*.

As far as I'm concerned, anyone who doesn't like *The Muppet Movie* doesn't have a soul — it's wonderful entertainment on so many levels. It's a movie about hope, pure and simple. This is laid out in the opening number, written by Paul Williams and sung by Jim Henson, a.k.a. Kermit the Frog.

The song begins by asking about the number of songs written about rainbows and the supposed pot of gold waiting on the other side. That opening question, posed with such melancholy, perfectly reflects the mood of Kermit's character. The lovely strings and the tinge of worry in Kermit's voice reveal a character facing an uphill battle in life. Content with his existence in the pond, dare he step outside of that comfort zone and pursue his desires in life? Is it worth the risk? After all, having big dreams dashed can be devastating. Still, the song offers that sense of hope I'm talking about. Kermit insists that someday the lovers and dreamers will uncover the rainbow connection, and he implies that when this happens things may get better. It is that dichotomy of hope and despair that made the song resonate with my young mind.

The Muppet Movie soundtrack was my very first contemporary record, and it scarred me for life. Since these were the days before VCRs, I couldn't go and watch the movie every night to remind myself that everything ends happily. I only had the music. Weeks were spent listening to "The Rainbow Connection" over and over. I felt Kermit's sadness and connected with his fear and doubt. It's the same fear and doubt, in fact, I still experience to this very day. I'm a member of the "lovers and dreamers" club, for sure, but at the time, I didn't know it. That's the remarkable thing about "The Rainbow Connection" for me; it touched a part of my soul that hadn't yet been awakened. It would be years before I figured out what I wanted to do with my life, but there I was, in 1979, already lost and unsure of myself.

Still, it's one of the loveliest songs to get lost in, and so great a melody that these concerns and worries Kermit sings about are easily forgotten as the chorus swells. Even now, as an adult, "The Rainbow Connection" can still take me back to my youth and those seemingly simpler times. Today, when I hear the opening banjo notes, I'm a child again. The worries of the day are forgotten for a brief time as I re-experience the simple joys of a nice song. I recall what it's like to be somewhat optimistic, what it's like to feel free and not worried all the time. This is the type of song I hope my children, Sophie and Jacob, latch onto and make one of their own.

I want them to always be full of the hope the song ultimately expresses, and I pray they don't experience the melancholy that I constantly go through, that part of my personality I fear I'll never be able to shed. Maybe it's that inherent melancholy that ironically keeps me feeling optimistic because whenever I'm feeling down and lonely, as if nothing is ever going to turn around, deep inside I believe there will be a light at the end of the tunnel, that some kind of treasure waits for me at the end of the rainbow. It may not be gold or money and may just be reassurance that things will work out. I have to keep that hope alive. I have to.

As easy as it would be to just cave in when the world seems to be coming down around me, I have to show the kids that you don't give up. Especially my son, Jacob. Living with a chronic illness, cystic fibrosis, he has to be a fighter.

"The Rainbow Connection" holds such a special place in my heart that I never bought it on CD. I need to hear the pops and hisses of my original LP before Kermit begins singing. Those imperfections bring me almost as much comfort as the banjo. Once upon a time, I dreamed big: I was going to be a huge star in Hollywood. Now, I'm content to be a huge star to my children, and my biggest dream is to be a better man and husband. Even if I'm not the same lover or dreamer that I was as a child, it's okay. I'm happy. And that's all you can ask for in life, isn't it?

Maybe it wasn't a basement where *you* discovered those songs that hold special meaning in your life. Maybe it was your bedroom or your car or a time when you went running while wearing headphones. Ultimately, it's not about *where* you heard the songs; it's about the songs themselves and how they've helped you get through life. One song. One moment in a lifetime of music.

The enduring quality of the music, then and now, is what makes a specific song special. A basement song has a place in your heart, and you can listen to it anytime and recall its specialness. Decades may pass and a familiar refrain will start playing, reminding you of where you were when it sank its hooks into you — as well as why you loved it and why it still affects you.

As you read this collection of some of my favorite Basement Songs, I hope that you can relate.

More importantly, I hope that you can enjoy.

THE B-52'S

"ROCK LOBSTER"

On a warm spring afternoon, with my school bag over my shoulder, I walked home from Forest Elementary School, shuffling my suede Thom McAn's along the sidewalk. It would be a few weeks until my mom dug the warm weather clothes out of the attic, so I was stuck in hot, stuffy attire, sweating profusely in corduroy pants and my thick down jacket. Drifting in the thoughts of my young third grade mind, probably thinking of that girl in my class I thought was "super pretty," it was the end of a typical school day which would conclude when I got home and I plopped down in a yellow rocker to watch *Battle of the Planets* and munch on raw spaghetti noodles (the only snack left in the house). That's when I heard *them* coming up behind me, and my life would change forever.

They approached, sounding like an army of two, their shoes kicking the pebbles and crumbling dried leaves on the ground.

Scrunch, scrunch, scrunch, scrunch.

In unison, they sang/chanted strange lyrics:

We were at the beach,
(Yeah, yeah)
Everybody had matching towels.

Spinning around, I saw two boys jogging toward me, both caught up in the exuberance of youth. I recognized one of them, Dave G. He was year ahead of me in school and had once belonged to my Cub Scout pack. With him was a lanky, blond kid I didn't recognize. Forest Elementary wasn't a large school; in general you knew everyone who went there, especially the students in the grades close to yours. But I'd never seen this guy before.

As they brushed past me, Dave looked my way and called out, "Hey, c'mon!"

With a shrug and the thrill of inclusion, I tagged along, the arms of my jacket *swish, swish, swish*-ing with every brush against my body. No introductions were made; there wasn't time! I quickly joined in with their pseudo-militaristic chant, even though I didn't know what the heck they were talking about:

We were at the beach
(Yeah, yeah)
Everybody had matching towels
Somebody went under the dock
And there they saw a rock
But it wasn't a rock…
It was a rock LOBSTER!

That's all they knew, so the three of us repeated this string of words over and over as we ran for another quarter mile. We reached the Black Path, a lonely stretch of a pavement that connected the school's immediate neighborhood and mine. Barely wide enough for two bicycles, the Black Path was more an afterthought than a reasonably planned route. The blacktop was always in shoddy shape, the weeds along the path always overgrown and menacing. I split off from Dave and the blond guy and headed home. As I left them I wore a broad smile. This bizarre run-in had made my day, as weird, spontaneous events were—and still are—wont to do.

It would be a couple of years before I learned the name of that song: catching a repeat of *Saturday Night Live*, I was amazed watching the B-52's performed the shit out of their cult hit "Rock Lobster."

Soon after my afternoon jog with Dave and his friend, he moved away. Our paths wouldn't cross again until his senior year of high school, when he returned to North Olmsted. As for the lanky blond guy, we met again the following summer when we played on the same team in the North Olmsted Soccer Organization. His name was Jack. After soccer and well into the next school year, we became fast friends, sharing the same tastes in music and sports. By high school, it was these common interests that landed us in the same cars that drove through town on Saturday nights or at the same parties where we watched each other's backs. By college, our friendship grew into something more unique. As the two of us challenged each other to become better men, Jack and I became confidants; more, we became brothers.

Years ago, I was honored to be the best man at Jack's wedding. During the rehearsal dinner, I shared this story of how we met. Underneath the laughs that we shared, Jack and I understood the significance of that day and how it changed both of our lives. Although we now live thousands of miles apart, our friendship remains as strong as ever, thanks in part to the miracle of the Internet.

Thirty years have passed since that afternoon in North Olmsted. I can't help but think of those two kids, strangers then, running alongside each other and the long journey they would travel together. That is how friendships are born: through chance encounters on the sidewalks of our youth. Not with formal introductions, but through the surf rock punk of a Georgia band and a rock lobster.

JOURNEY
ESCAPE

We all have that one friend, that person you've known for so long that you can't recall how the two of you first met. They were just always there – a part of your life. For me, that person was Matt. We met sometime in the first grade and quickly began hanging out. I'd often stop in his house after school for a snack or to check out his room full of toys, like the Maskatron (enemy of the Six Million Dollar Man) action figure that came with three interchangeable faces, or to leaf through his latest issues of *Mad Magazine* or *Cracked.* Throughout our formative years, the two of us were like siblings. We loved each other and because of that love we fought, had misunderstandings, hurt each other and went through periods in which we didn't speak. Yet, each time we drifted apart, there was a comfort of knowing that the other was around whenever needed.

Sixth grade was a year of growing pains and awkwardness, as puberty reared its inevitable head. Over the summer, I had grown taller than anyone in my class, my voice sank drastically, I shaved for the first time, began using deodorant and had hair sprouting out of places I wasn't prepared to deal with. With my friend Jack moving on to the seventh grade, I was oblivious to the great friendship I had in Matt. Looking back, I will always regret the need be "accepted" by the popular cliques. I believe it had something to do with being an ASS kid.

In the autumn of 1981, I was entering my second year in an "Advanced Study Program" (ASP), an experimental academic program which selected certain "advanced" students from grades 3-6 and placed them all in one separate pod classroom. It often felt like we were miles away from the rest of the student population instead of simply on the other end of the school. All of the "cool" kids — kids I used to hang around with — labeled us ASP students the "ASS" students.

Matt understood that you can still have a good time even if you're not one of the cool kids. I began to appreciate his outlook early in the year. That September, most of the sixth graders from Forest Elementary attended a weeklong camping trip at the Mohican outdoor camp in central Ohio. We slept in cabins, went on hikes, canoed and watched chickens get their heads cut off for dinner. Unfortunately, Matt didn't go, so I spent that week trying to fit in with some of the same guys who were calling me an ASS kid. For the most part, I tried to remain inconspicuous, though it's hard to do that when you're freakin' Goliath. The worst time of the week came during mandatory showers in the open stalls of the bathroom.

Unbeknownst to me, my mother had inadvertently packed a *hand* towel for me to dry off with. I did all that I could to keep my back turned and go unnoticed. I was a hairy monster compared to some of the other guys and it didn't take long for one kid to notice me and snidely remark, "You *would* have pubes." I dried off to snickers and stares and got the hell out of there. I felt like a social outcast, a mutant from the X-Men.

At the end of the week, we returned to the school to wait for our parents. I entered the ASP classroom to find Matt, sitting on the floor with his back against the wall and his knees bent. He looked up at me and smiled. A huge sense of relief came over me, and I felt that the first year of puberty wasn't going to be so bad as long as I had my oldest friend by my side. I eventually confided in him about the shower incident. Coming to my defense, he told me that should it ever come up again, I should have a witty comeback ready to fire, something like "At least I *have* pubes!" We both thought the phrase was hilarious, but I never got to use it.

From that day forward, we were inseparable. Together we waded through the boring topics our teachers forced upon us and obsessed over the books of Stephen King, *Fangoria* magazine, *The Twilight Zone,* and the music of Journey. Of course, everyone in the world loved Journey in 1981. That July, the San Francisco rock band catapulted to superstardom with the release of *Escape*, their bestselling album that included the power ballad, "Open Arms," as well as the enduring single, "Don't Stop Believin'. "

Matt and I had been fans of the band before *Escape* conquered the world. He owned earlier records *Infinity* and *Captured*, while I had the 45 single of "Any Way You Want It" and a cassette copy of someone's scratched *Evolution* LP. By Christmastime, I had *Escape* on LP and Matt had the tape. He really missed out, though, for the cover art by Stanley Mouse needed to be held so that you could run your fingers over the raised edges of the scarab spaceship and shattering egg that adorned it. Journey's rise to world domination happened to coincide with my takeover of the family basement. My older sister, Beth, was away at college, my brother, Budd, was spending less time at home as he became more sociable, and my younger sister, Heidi, was content spending upstairs with her toys. So it was easy for me to seclude myself downstairs and listen to *Escape*. During this period, I also became committed about playing the drums. Journey's drummer, Steve Smith, was a perfect role model: Any style of music came easy to him, and he knew how to play in the groove. As a result of playing along with Smith, my drumming chops improved, although to this date, I still mess up the unusual rhythm of "Don't Stop Believin'. "

Despite my ambitions to become a better drummer and my affinity for the album's cool visuals, it was simply the music that kept me coming back to *Escape*. The production isn't overly slick, and the harder-edged songs have a rough quality that places the listener directly in the studio with the band. In my opinion, there isn't a weak track on this album. Side one includes "Don't Stop Believin'," the hard rocking "Stone in Love," "Who's Crying Now," another hit that features a majestic solo by guitarist Neal Schon, and "Still They Ride," which ranks at the top of my favorite Journey songs. This ballad features fine piano work by Jonathan Cain, lead singer Steve Perry channeling his idol, Sam Cooke, and a solo by Schon so graceful, you can almost feel the calluses in Schon's fingers crack as he pours all he's got into those notes.

Side two has a much harder driving selection of songs, perhaps a response from Schon to the abundance of pop-friendly singles on the first side. The title track contains the best qualities of mainstream music from the early '80s: It's melodic, full of tempo variations and contains lyrics that speak of the hopes and dreams of teens and adults alike. Buried near the end of the album is the heartbreaking "Mother, Father," a song about a broken family. When we were kids, I never understood why this song spoke to Matt, why he loved it. Not until we were in our 30's, several drinks into a night on the town, did he reveal his reasons. It took him all of those years to confide in me what had been bearing down on him his entire life. I guess there are just some things we don't share with other people, not even the ones we love. Whenever I hear this song, I can only think of him.

Matt and I spent the spring of 1982 trying to convince our parents to take us to the Greg Kihn/Journey show at the Richfield Coliseum. None of them wanted to step near that smoky dungeon of potheads and loud guitars. Bummed as we were, a year later we finally got to see the band live. Matt's mom relented and took us to see Journey, as they toured in support of the follow-up album, *Frontiers*. The opening act was an up-and-coming Canadian rocker named Bryan Adams. Although our seats were behind the stage, the concert was a dream come true.

Looking back on those early years of adolescence, I hope to use my experiences to help steer my children from the doubts and sadness that I went through. I'm not sure I'll be able to do that, but I'll try.

Matt and I remained close throughout high school and college. During the '90s, our lives went in vastly different directions. I found the love of my life, got married and moved to Los Angeles. Matt moved to Seattle, lived alone, and easily slipped into the Bohemian scene. Just like the siblings we had become, the two of us were going through a silent period as the new century rolled around. Matt passed away in 2005 from complications of diabetes. It still saddens me that we weren't speaking when he died, two stubborn men unwilling to pick up the damn phone. Immediately following his death, I wondered if he still had a small place in his heart for Journey, even though his musical tastes had become more esoteric and dark. I found out from his brother that shortly before dying, Matt had attended a Journey concert. Hopefully they played "Mother, Father" that night. If they did, I know he would have been happy, and he would have been thinking about the good times we had together all those years before.

THE WHO
"BABA O'RILEY"

Late in 1984 my dad bought a used 1978 Oldsmobile Delta 88. The car was originally blue with a white vinyl top, but years of inclement weather had taken its toll. The paint had long faded and been replaced with brown rust spots, and the vinyl was gray with decay. The extent of the rust damage to the Delta 88 wasn't revealed until the first thunderstorm, when the roof leaked and the seats became waterlogged. That winter, my leg was in a brace following knee surgery, so there wasn't much I could do to correct this problem. My father seemed content with the car the way it was. The following spring, however, with my leg close to normal, I got fed up with sitting in wet spots and tore off the vinyl covering on the exterior of the roof.

Rust had eaten away at the metal, leaving four gaping holes in the center and along the edge where the roof connected to the siding. Even though I was months away from my driver's license, I knew that this rolling monster would eventually become the vehicle I drove on dates or for cruising around town. If something was going to be done to correct the problem, it would be up to me. With the help of a tub of Bondo auto repair putty, I filled in the holes and sealed the gaps in the roof. The workmanship was amateurish at best, but at least it wouldn't look like I had wet myself whenever I climbed out of the car on a rainy day.

The Delta 88 remained a mismatched, ugly monstrosity well into the early months of my driving life. Sometime in the spring of '86, I had an idea: I could paint a flag on the roof of the car! The thought was a whim, and I doubted that my father would even consider it; after all, he had to drive around town in the car. Still, I decided to give it a shot and, much to my surprise, when I asked his permission, he didn't scowl at me. Instead, he asked me what flag I had in mind.

Visions of *The Dukes of Hazzard* filled my head, and I suggested the Confederate flag. He adamantly said "No." He had taught in Georgia during the '60s, and the racism he saw firsthand still left a sour taste in his mouth. That flag was an ugly reminder of the past, and he wasn't about to display it on his car.

Thinking fast, I spat out, "How about the Union Jack?"

He thought a moment. "The flag of England?" I shrugged as if to say, sure. He curled his lower lip in approval and simply said "Okay." A couple of weeks later the Bondo was covered with the blue, red and white flag of Great Britain. It wasn't perfect, but close enough.

The Whomobile was born.

Credit is due to my close friend, Sally, who gave the car its name. Soon after she dubbed it the Whomobile, I painted the moniker in twelve-inch white letters along the front edge of the hood, just below the ornament. Sometime later I received a mysterious note from a stranger, placed on the windshield. This obvious fan of the car simply wrote, "Who the fuck are you?" I decided to ask the same question to cars following me (sans the profanity) by painting it in massive letters on the back of the car. Mind you, these additions were done without consulting my parents. They never said a word, though. In truth, I believe my dad enjoyed being seen in the Whomobile.

I wish I could describe the many crazy adventures that took place in the Whomobile, but the reality is there weren't many. Mostly it was "the car," a symbol of individuality amongst my friends. It was a part of my image and became a symbol of who I was. And yes, I liked the thought of being perceived as "cool." Trust me, I was not.

My most vivid memories of the Whomobile involve the numerous midnight treks through the Cleveland Metroparks with Jack or Matt riding shotgun. Those trips sometimes involved deep personal conversations, and sometimes they involved long stretches of silence while we listened to the radio. Classic rock had just become a popular format, and The Who was receiving a career resurgence. At that time, Jack was enraptured with *Quadrophenia,* while I preferred *Tommy*. However, we both agreed upon *Who's Next*, the band's masterpiece, which included one of their signature songs, "Baba O'Riley." To this day, the majesty of that composition, with its instantaneously recognizable synthesizer intro and Pete Townshend's thunderous guitar chords, always brings chills along my spine. And when Roger Daltrey lets out his guttural scream at the end, I'm a kid again; I feel like I did back then, part of something larger than myself.

There were many dates in that car. The front seat was large enough to make out without worrying about getting a cramp in your arm. And the backseat… well, the backseat was cozy. Now, I was no Don Juan in high school, but I had my share of girlfriends, and I had my share of broken hearts. During the most important breakups and epiphanies, the Whomobile was handy to take for a spin and clear my head.

The August before my senior year I learned that *the girl*, the one for whom I'd pined for nearly a year, had expressed an interest in me. This was a dream come true. The evening I found out, I rushed home from work to call Jack with the fantastic news. So excited was I that as soon as I pulled in our driveway, I opened the door and jumped out…without shutting off the car! The Whomobile rolled forward into the bushes and came within inches of running into the house. Luckily, I was able to slam on the brakes before disaster. No matter, my elation dampened any fears of vegetation damage. The Whomobile was there for the beginning of this important relationship, and its final gasp was a harbinger of everything crashing to an end.

The Wednesday before Thanksgiving in 1987, I drove through the main drag of North Olmsted as gray skies tempted rain. While idling at a red light, the car lurched forward, clinked and squeaked, then died in the middle of an intersection. I was able to crank the wheels and coast into a nearby parking lot, where the Whomobile came to a final halt. Later on, as a tow truck hauled the car off to a mechanic's garage, I didn't realize that that would be the last time I saw the Whomobile. It was appropriate that I was driving the car that afternoon; it was appropriate that I was with the dying beast as it left this world. A week later, my folks bought a wretched conversion van with bucket seats, curtains and a pull out bed in the back. I had no use for this thing. It had no history. It was just a car.

The same week the van was purchased, that girl of my dreams walked into the video store where I worked and told me that her family was moving. Suddenly, I was without my heart and my armor. My car was gone and by January, so was my girl.

It took a long time to get over both losses. Many long, lonely nights spent in the basement listening to sad songs by Springsteen couldn't fill the void in my heart. And without the Whomobile, it didn't feel the same roaming the streets of my town. First love prepares you for great things in life; first love shows you the possibilities of the wonder of love. Yet, it also sets you up for heartbreak. When you lose that first love, whether it's a girl or a car, you're never the same. When the cold winter blues finally melted away, I climbed out of the basement a little more mature and prepared to move on. I was ready to rock again. I may not have been a part of some teenage wasteland, but I wanted to travel south cross land and not look back.

You can let the pain control you, or you can use it to make you a better person. For all the love I felt for that girl, it wasn't meant to be. I have no regrets because my life's path was heading toward my wife, Julie, and the incredible life we would have. Still, what I wouldn't give for just one more ride around the block in the Whomobile, with the windows rolled down and "Baba O'Riley" blasting from the speakers.

THE POLICE
"WRAPPED AROUND YOUR FINGER"

During the summer of 1986 I was the drummer in a garage band that actually had gigs. By this point I had my own drum set, a white, eight-piece Rogers kit that I hauled from North Olmsted to neighboring Bay Village every time we rehearsed. Our repertoire was comprised mostly of new and popular college radio tunes, including the Police hit, "Message in a Bottle." The thrill of that song inspired me to dig deeper into the Police catalog and come to appreciate the musicianship of Police drummer, Stewart Copeland. His style appealed to me because his playing, while precise, maintained a looseness that countered the perfectionism of Police bassist/singer, Sting, and the intricate guitar work of Andy Summers. Additionally, Copeland had a knack for making the simplest drum fills sound so damn cool.

Take "Wrapped Around Your Finger" from *Synchronicity*. It's an uncomplicated song: bass and rim shot during the verses, then a driving beat introducing the snare during the choruses. Copeland maintains this pattern throughout the track until just before the final chorus. Then, playing one of my favorite drum licks of all time, he throws out a fill that is merely snare, high hat and a bass drum –

Daka tss tss, daka tss tss, boom GAT!

– and then the final chorus. So simple, yet it announces the song's big finish with authority (to borrow from *Bull Durham*). I must have played "Wrapped Around Your Finger" over a hundred times, wearing down the grooves of my younger sister's vinyl copy of *Synchronicity*.

Because I was in that band, I found leverage to miss out on the yearly Malchus summer vacation with my parents and sister. We had a couple gigs lined up for the two weeks my folks wanted to leave town and being a "professional," I wasn't going to let my band down. Remarkably, my parents found virtue in my argument and agreed to let me stay home with my brother (about to enter his senior year of college), acting as the adult chaperone. What that meant was that I'd essentially have the house to myself since Budd was always working or out with his friends. What this meant to Matt was that he, too, would have a place to live, parent-free, for two weeks.

At that time, I was dating a girl named…we'll call her "Sandy." I really had the hots for Sandy and figured that an empty house would be the ideal location to make my move. The night I decided to make that move was a Wednesday, I believe. Budd was gone somewhere and I had the house to myself.

Well, not exactly.

See, Matt wanted to hang out that night, in the house, regardless of whether or not I was there. Being the good friend that I was, I saw no problem with this. As long as he stayed in the basement and kept it down, I could still get it on with Sandy.

Around 10 p.m. Sandy and I had just finished watching some movie. I have no clue what it was because the movie was the furthest thing from my mind. With the lights already out (because of the movie, right?), I didn't have to be coy. When we started kissing, I convinced Sandy that it would be much more comfortable if we snuggled on the pulled-out futon couch. Moments later we were pressed against each other's bodies, our snug OP shorts and Polo shirts causing friction. I was *certain* that I was going to score.

Oh, did I forget to say that for the duration of the movie, Matt sat silently in the basement pounding a six-pack of Genesee?

Sandy and I begin to move past the French kissing phase and get a little more passionate. It was getting late, so I made the bold choice to forgo getting in her shirt. I moved my hand up the back of her thigh, instead. Mind you, Sandy was wearing late '80s short shorts so just reaching their hem meant that I was practically home free. My fingers crept closer and closer when suddenly…we hear the Police blaring from the basement and Matt singing along with them.

Despite Sandy's initial giggles, we went back to kissing. Lacking in confidence and unsure of what the correct etiquette was for copping a feel, I started all over again, working my way up the back of her thigh, in hopes of getting up the back of her shorts and then working my way around front. I crept my hand back up. Was I even kissing her? I guess. My mind was elsewhere. Soon…TRIUMPH! I got my fingers up the back of her shorts and brushed the seam of her cotton underwear. Just as I was about to begin my next move…we hear Matt attempting to play the drums.

There is nothing worse than a drunk person who doesn't know how to play the drums…trying to play the drums.

Sandy laughed out loud. "What is he doing? Should we go check?"

"NO!" I exclaimed. "I mean, *I'll* go see what's up."

I jumped up, opened the basement door and walked down the twenty-four steps to the basement, where Matt was trying to play along with the Police. We spoke in hushed tones.

"Dude!" I said to him.

"Dude," he replied. "What are you doing down here? Where's Sandy?"

"She's upstairs. What are YOU doing down here, dude? Holy…did you drink that whole six-pack?"

"Nope. Only four."

I rolled my eyes. "Keep it down. Sandy and I are…I'm trying to…"

"Oh. OH! Right. Sorry."

He gave me a thumbs-up and I ran back up the twenty-four steps.

Sandy and I kissed. I moved my hand up her thigh. I got up the back of her shorts. I actually slid my pinky under her underwear and I felt her butt. I. Was. Going. To. Score.

And then…we heard the off-key, warbled vocals of a drunk Matt singing the chorus of "Wrapped Around Your Finger."

Sandy burst out in laughter. In my head I was screaming! Once again, I jumped up and ran down the twenty-four steps, this time cursing his name with each step. Matt was on the couch, a new beer in hand.

"Dude!"

"What? Oh, shit. Did you hear me? Sorry." He put his finger to his lips, as if to say, "Shh."

I nodded and RAN back up the steps, two at a time.

Sandy was now glancing through a magazine. I leapt back beside her. We kissed. I moved my hand. Got it up the back of her shorts. Under the seam of the underwear. My OP shorts were about to burst!

Matt CRASHED in the basement, bringing down a cymbal.

We heard a meek, "Ouch."

Steam coming from my ears, I went over to the basement door and opened it with a slow hand. A small part of me prayed that he'd decapitated himself with the cymbal. I walked down the steps and found him sprawled out on the floor, a crashed cymbal next to him.

"I fell."

On cue, Stewart Copeland announced the end of my evening with authority.

Daka tss tss, daka tss tss, boom GAT!

Sandy called out from the top of the stairwell, "I think I should go." I forced a smile and "Wrapped Around Your Finger" played off to its end.

I trudged up those damn twenty-four steps and led Sandy out to the car. By the time I'd returned from driving her home some twenty minutes later, Matt was passed out. He looked so innocent, sleeping like a baby. And as much as I was mad at him twenty minutes earlier, I couldn't help but laugh. Girlfriends came and went in those days. But the friendship I had with Matt was more important. I'd give him hell, but what else could I do? He was my best friend.

TOM WAITS
"KENTUCKY AVENUE"

The acid-drenched voice of Tom Waits crackled from the small record player in the corner of the classroom. As students filed into the classroom for Mr. Denman's 12th grade AP English, the singer's voice was difficult to understand. The deteriorating vinyl, coupled with the commotion of my classmates, made this song sound like it had been recorded in another century. Denman was notorious for treating his LP's like shit. On any given day you were likely to find a stack of records, out of their sleeves, resting on the floor near the heater. Any collector would have found it appalling. I thought it was a little rebellious and cool. His AP English class was really a course in pop culture. He transformed what could have been a tedious year of English literature into an excursion in books, music, film, theater and history. This included introducing his naïve students to critically adored yet publicly ignored artists like Waits.

On this day, he had chosen "Kentucky Avenue" from Waits' 1978 album, *Blue Valentine.* After the bell rang and the class settled, Denman let the song play to its completion. Even though I could barely figure out what Waits was singing about, I sat there spellbound and was haunted by the melody for the rest of the day. Years later, while hanging out with Matt, he pulled out *Blue Valentine* and played the song, allowing me, for the first time, to decipher Waits poignant song.

Waits sings with an abrasive honesty that has you wondering if he's singing about someone from his own youth. A deep pain rises up from underneath his reflections of childhood. He misleads us in the early verses, having us believe that the song is just a flashback of youth gone wild. By the end, the lyrics reveal the true story:

I'll take a rusty nail and scratch your initials on my arm
And I'll show you how to sneak up on the roof of the drugstore
Take the spokes from your wheelchair
And a magpie's wings
And tie 'em to your shoulders and your feet
I'll steal a hacksaw from my dad
And cut the braces off your legs
And we'll bury them tonight in the cornfield

This isn't a story about two punks: It's a song about two friends, or perhaps siblings, one of whom is disabled. The other is doing everything within his power to make his companion feel "normal," as if there were such a thing.

Memories of the many misadventures Matt and I shared arise whenever I take a ride down "Kentucky Avenue," in particular the time we shoplifted comic books from the convenience store near the city water tower. We fled the store with about twenty books stuffed underneath our shirts. Riding away on our bikes, we sped through the crosswalk of a busy intersection when the comics spilled out and onto the street. The two of us scrambled to pick up the books and raced away, scared shitless. Later, laughing at ourselves, we felt like bad boys, though we were the farthest thing from it. Those comic books helped build the foundation of our relationship; we studied the art and read the stories countless times. In my backyard, we'd imagine ourselves as Green Lantern or Superman, joining forces to defeat evil and save the world (getting the girl wasn't so important back then). A couple of years later, we traced over the pages of those comics, trying to learn how to draw the images of the muscle-bound heroes we wanted to be.

I store these memories in my hip pocket for quick access during those times when all I can recall are the sad note on which our friendship ended. Once we were young; once, we loved each other like brothers.

I also think of my son, Jacob, whenever I listen to "Kentucky Avenue." He is getting older, asking questions about his disease and noticing that no one else he knows has cystic fibrosis. I fear for him. I don't want the monster living inside his body to prevent him from having both good and bad childhood experiences, like the ones I had. I want him to feel as "normal" as the other kids in his class. I believe that all parents want this for their children; all parents hope that their children will have wonderful lives growing up. But all parents also fear that something terrible may happen to their son or daughter. Oh, we may not talk about it, but the fear is there. For me that fear is ever-present — each morning when Jacob does his breathing treatments and every time I hear him cough.

If I could get a hacksaw and cut away the cystic fibrosis from Jacob's life, I would do it in a heartbeat.

One of the greatest lessons I took away from that AP English class was *carpe diem*: to live life to the fullest every day we're alive. We did our best, Matt and I. We will never again run wild like the kids we were, and the next time we'll be able to laugh at each other's mistakes is when we're side-by-side in Heaven. For Jacob, I hope to instill in him the same philosophy taught to me by my great teacher, Mr. Denman, and I will do all that I can to ensure that he can make mistakes and experience life.

I will do everything I can to make sure Jacob can someday take a trip down his own Kentucky Avenue and sing about it.

PINK FLOYD
"ON THE TURNING AWAY"

Through the eyes of my son, I've been reliving a part of my youth in the form of colorful costumed superheroes from cartoons and the pages of comic books. His sister, Sophie, and mom have no enthusiasm whatsoever for this stuff, so Jacob and I bond over the muscle-bound humans out to save the world. With equal parts fascination and wonder, the two of us leaf through my musty old comics from the '80s and the glossy new ones we buy once a month.

My personal interest began as a child, around Jacob's age, when my parents purchased me the oversized graphic novel *Superman vs. Wonder Woman*. I read it so many times the pages are in tatters. From that point on, I was obsessed with all of the big guns like Spider-Man, Daredevil, Superman and Green Arrow. My favorite adventures always involved that group of outcasts, the Uncanny X-Men. Throughout my adolescence, I bought most of my X-Men comics at the Convenient Food Mart, located next door to the music studio where I took drum lessons. During the short period of time between when my lesson ended and when my father would pick me up, I'd peruse the comic books displayed in one of those spinning metal racks that always squeaked when you turned it. With any change I could scrounge from the sofa cushions or whatever I "acquired" from my dad's dresser, my monthly dose of mutant mayhem would always get snuck into the house and immediately taken to the basement, as if I were carrying a *Playboy* or something worse.

I'm unsure where this feeling that reading comic books was an illicit, depraved hobby came from, but it stayed with me throughout my teens. By the time I was in high school, driving myself to drum lessons and paying for my comics with my own cash, I believe it was the ongoing fear of looking childish that kept me from being open about my passion for comics. When I was supposed to be poring over the works of Dostoyevsky, Faulkner and Voltaire, I didn't want my friends to know I was more interested in Chris Claremont, Alan Moore and Frank Miller. The pull of the X-Men was the action, drama and romance, escapism primarily. Yet the central themes I've always identified with (like brotherhood, loyalty, tolerance and redemption) were ever-present. Ironically, many of these same themes were found in the novels I was reading by those classic authors I mentioned.

In early '88, it was comfort more than anything else that I was seeking. During that winter I holed myself up in the basement to mope about a broken heart and listen to Bruce Springsteen's heartbreaking album, *Tunnel of Love.* My one pleasure was delving into the X-Men saga "Fall of the Mutants." In this epic story, Storm, Rogue, Wolverine and their teammates sacrifice their lives to defeat an evil spirit unleashed on our world. As I read each issue several times over, my musical accompaniment on my fanboy journey was Pink Floyd's 1987 comeback LP, *A Momentary Lapse of Reason.*

The apocalyptic feel and melancholy tone of that album, particularly "On the Turning Away," reflected the sadness of the X-Men facing down death for a world that doesn't particularly like them because they are different. That music became so intertwined with the story that I couldn't listen to the record otherwise; it didn't have the same impact on me without the words of Claremont and the art of Mark Silvestri.

Twenty years later, that same artwork is unappealing to me; I find it too static and rough. And I can barely listen to *A Momentary Lapse of Reason* anymore, finding its '80s production values too bombastic. Yet, "On the Turning Away" holds up. It begins quietly, like any good story, inviting you into the plot and then gradually builds until the climactic finale. Yes, the drums sound like cannons going off, and there are moments that could be outtakes from Pink Floyd's epic record, *The Wall,* but David Gilmour sings with sincerity and, as usual, his guitar playing is impeccable.

When Jacob discovered my favorite mutant superheroes through their animated adventures on television, we started reading some of my old comics together. If you can imagine a grown man sitting on a couch with his seven-year-old snuggled up next to him, trying to explain why people hate the X-Men even though they're heroes, then you'll have imagined many nights in our household. If only I could get him to listen to Floyd with me, then my life will have come full circle. I guess there's still time.

Lately, Jake has struggled with being the only kid he knows with cystic fibrosis. Besides the physical challenges of taking multiple medicines and having your chest pounded daily by a machine, there is the emotional aspect that we without the disease have difficulty understanding. CF is an illness for which there is no cure, so he will live with these treatments and medicines and the thought of being different his whole life.

One evening, we discussed how the X-Men got their powers:

"They were born with them," I explained.

"Do they like their powers?" he asked.

"If most of them had their way, they wish they'd never been born with their mutant powers."

It dawned on me that Jacob is like his favorite heroes, born with something he doesn't want, but bravely making the best of it. This little boy inspires me in ways no one ever has. When I tell him he's my hero, he doesn't really understand; he usually laughs and says, "Daddy, I'm not a hero. I don't have super powers."

Jake may not be able to walk through walls or disappear in a cloud of brimstone, and he may not be able to move solid objects with his thoughts or soar through the air on wings growing out of his back. But he has the strength of a thousand men, and he could teach those characters in the comics a thing or two about courage.

BRUCE HORNSBY & THE RANGE
"THE OLD PLAYGROUND"

The kid from Maple School broke away and dribbled down the court. Just five steps ahead of me, he had a wide-open lane for an easy lay-up. As he lifted the ball for his shot, I plowed into him, sending the two of us into the padding of the gym wall. The ref blew the whistle on me, but I didn't care. I knew this guy would never make his free throws. I had saved my team two points.

And there you have the crowning moment of my glory days on the Chestnut Elementary seventh-grade basketball team.

I suck at round ball, although it took me awhile to admit it. When the seventh-grade coach took me aside to ask why I wanted to be on the basketball team, subtly implying that I would never get playing time because, yes, I was terrible, I only got more determined to prove him wrong. Nope, he was right, and I never joined the basketball team again. Still, for a couple years after that single season of pre-teen basketball, I lived with the delusion that those four months qualified me to hold my own on the court. What was I thinking? I'm a hack. I'm not even a good hack; I foul out of games in the first quarter — or I would, if I still tried to play basketball.

Jack was on the varsity team in high school, so I spent a great deal of time in his driveway trying to guard him as he drove to the basket around me, or over me, or he just did a fade-away jumper while I dove at him with my arms flapping like a lame pigeon. Jack nearly always made his shot. Sometimes I'd get a hand on the ball, or his wrist, or his back, or in his face. He'd never complain. In fact, he'd even throw out the occasional, "Nice D." True friends will do that — prop you up when it's clear that you're just not very good.

It seems like whenever we weren't hanging out in the basement or cruising around in the Whomobile, Jack and I were tossing a basketball at his hoop while a tape deck spun the Who, the Kinks or the Blues Brothers. Since there wasn't much of a game being played, the two of us would joke around or talk about everyday events. I also did my best to wow him with my encyclopedic knowledge of useless pop culture information. Then there were days when we would reveal our fears and concerns about girlfriends, school, or what the future held for us. Whether the biting cold day of autumn, or the cool, sunny spring, I treasure those afternoons in North Olmsted.

During the summer of '89, Jack and I were in our second year with the North Olmsted Board of Education college maintenance crew, painting the interiors and exteriors of schools, mowing lawns and performing whatever menial labor the bosses had lined up for us. Our cohort, Jeff, was back from Purdue, as was Stacey, our crew chief, one of the nicest people I've ever met. Along with Jack, the other two had also played basketball in high school. During our breaks we would play pickup games on the elementary school playgrounds or in the high school gym. I held my own: didn't make many shots, but heard a lot of "Nice D" from the other guys.

When I hear a rubber ball smack against pavement, giving off that high-pitched whine, or sneakers squeak on a hardwood floor, images of my friends' faces are conjured in my head. I can see and hear the determination, the petty arguments, the high-fives and the camaraderie.

Besides the gyms and driveways of my childhood, "The Old Playground" can also be found on side two of Bruce Hornsby and the Range's sophomore effort, *Scenes from the Southside.* My cassette of the album received significant play during the sticky, hot summer days of 1989, as Jeff and I were both Bruce Hornsby fans. The song is an ode to the game Hornsby loves, combining the hip-hop beats you'd expect to hear in the background of an inner city basketball game with the down-home, jam-band style of his brightest songs. It's rare to hear a jazzy, piano-based song about basketball in rock and roll. Girls, yes. Cars, you bet. Even dead dogs have a slew of songs devoted to them. Hornsby's fervor comes through loud and clear, making it one of his most delightful numbers. That must be why "The Old Playground" retains its magic to me. Hearing those opening synth beats, Hornsby's syncopated solo, and Hornsby's lines about pickup games and playground rules make me wish I could go back to the old playground for one more go around and one last chance to see my buddy, Jeff.

Last year we bought a basketball hoop for Sophie and Jacob. It sits in our driveway right outside the front door. I have no delusions that either of our children will want to play basketball (if they do, I'm sure they'll excel at it, unlike their father). The hoop is there for fun. On nights when it's not too hot, I'll sometimes play a game of HORSE with Sophie or lift Jacob high in the air so he can slam-dunk the ball. There are times when I'll stand just inside the house and hear Sophie outside with her friends, shooting baskets and talking about how their day was. In those moments, I imagine the future when Sophie or Jacob are playing one-on-one with their best friends, and an iPod is playing music in the background.

I imagine them revealing their fears and concerns as only friends can do and telling each other, "Nice D."

THEY MIGHT BE GIANTS
"ANA NG"

If you should find yourself in North Olmsted, Ohio with a few extra minutes, you can drive past the high school. There, if you know where to look, you'll find a brown brick, perfectly centered between two windows on the way to the soccer practice field at the back of the school. Because it is brown, this brick blends in nicely with the rest of the orange and tan skin of the school. That layer of burnt umber, oil-based paint was applied to the wall on a humid, scorching afternoon in August 1990. At the tail-end of my time working on the North Olmsted Board of Education summer maintenance crew, I decided to leave my mark on the school in which I grew up and started the path to adulthood.

For three years, I worked alongside a group of college guys my age and a staff of men in their 40's and 50's ("lifers" as we called them) who were the full-time maintenance crew for the school system. Each year, our summers were spent sweating our asses off in the Ohio heat, primarily painting classrooms and the exterior trim of the schools. My friend Jeff landed me the job, and I convinced him to persuade Mike Clancy, the head of the Maintenance Department, to hire Jack, too. Like I said, I matured during that period. I learned how to be a better friend, an okay boyfriend (which would provide me with the lessons to be a good husband someday) and a halfway decent painter. Those laborious days were full of *Diner*-esque conversations, lazy, introspective moments and a lot of good music playing from my Emerson dual cassette boom box. Although there were many songs I grew to love during that time, many of those tunes hold only nostalgic value to me these days. However, one song remains one of my favorites, and it's one that I would include in my personal Top Ten: "Ana Ng" by They Might Be Giants.

In 1988, having graduated from high school, I anxiously awaited the fall and what Bowling Green State University had in store for me. I hoped to learn everything I needed to know about becoming a writer and a filmmaker. I knew the road was going to be long and tough, and that's where my anxiety came from. Was I up to this challenge? What if everything I tried to do was shit? What if I failed and wound up back in Ohio for the rest of my life? At that age, there was nothing worse, to me, than failing and winding up living with my parents. On top of all of this, I was still heartbroken from my high school sweetheart moving away and the feeble attempt at making a long distance relationship work crumbling miserably. To paraphrase Crash Davis, I was "dealing with a lot of shit there."

Luckily, Jack, my best friend and the one guy I looked up to more than my brother, was returning from his freshman year at UNC. I was able to tap into his knowledge and listen to his stories of what to expect: girls, parties, long nights theorizing and drinking, hard classes, dickhead teachers, if you're lucky a solid roommate and (if you're lucky) some new, good friends. There was also independence, freedom, and of course, there was the music.

College radio was in its heyday, featuring the Cure, Echo and the Bunnymen, INXS, the Minutemen, the 'Mats and so many more there isn't enough space. One of the albums Jack was hooked on was *Lincoln,* by a couple of guys named John who hailed from New York. John Flansburgh and John Linnell wrote quirky, offbeat songs that fit into no particular style. At that point in the '80s they still played all of the instruments on their songs, which ranged from accordion to saxophone to guitar. I had never heard They Might Be Giants (TMBG) before that summer, but Jack's enthusiasm for *Lincoln* was infectious. The moment the guitar and drum machine of "Ana Ng" charged into my ears, my life changed. There is something so hypnotic about the driving music: it makes you want to bounce up and down, bobbing your head like one of the characters in the *Peanuts* cartoons. Linnell's nasal delivery carries a hint of sadness that this woman, Ana, is not his. Either he's lost her love or it was never his to begin with, that's a question left for us to decide.

I'll be honest: To this day I barely have a clue what the hell he's singing about. I do believe it involves a failed relationship. The coolly-delivered spoken words in the middle of the song by a woman reinforce this thought. She doesn't want the world, only her lover's portion. The bitterness of that line always affected me. What happened to this couple, and how do I avoid that happening to me? I would soon learn that you can't avoid unhappy endings to relationships that were never meant to be.

Knowing that it was a drum machine should have turned off the drummer in me. But learning that these two New York guys had played all the instruments and programmed the drum machine intrigued me. Their D.I.Y. approach inspired me and still does to this day. I thought, "If these two guys can produce a melancholic masterpiece, imagine what I might achieve some day." That thinking helped me get through the making of my film, *King's Highway* and just about anything I've written. And that was, perhaps, one of the most important lessons I learned over the course of those three summers: The possibilities of the future are endless.

Each summer I was on the paint crew, and each subsequent summer after that, I have returned to "Ana Ng." It is the only appropriate way I know how to kick off the season. Even after the release of TMBG's breakthrough album, *Flood*, in 1990, if I didn't hear "Ana Ng" at least 70-100 times, I felt incomplete. It became an anthem for three of the best years of my young adulthood. My life would be empty without the time I spent wasting away those days in North Olmsted. Most important, my friendship with Jack grew into brotherhood over that time; if only for that, I am grateful. I believe that is why I chose to paint the brick. In 1991, Jack would graduate, and I would be on an internship in California. 1990 was our last summer of seeing each other every morning, calling one another in the afternoon and just getting together to do nothing but shoot hoops or cruise through the valley. As we've gotten older, there are no more days like that, which makes periodic visits that Jack bestows upon us all the more special.

There were actually three bricks painted, one at each school we worked at: Chestnut Elementary, the middle school and the high school. I have no clue where the other two brown bricks are located. I believe they are high up, near the roof, and hidden from sight. The day we decided to paint the high school brick was a typical afternoon. Sweltering, dripping heat. I'm sure our clothes stank of sweat, alcohol from the night before, grime from not showering and paint fumes. Jack and I were separated from the rest of the crew, on a scaffold. We were in the wide open, yet we couldn't have been more alone. With no one around, it suddenly struck me to paint that brick. "We should paint one here," I must have said. Jack, ever the cautious one, likely replied with an unsure, "Okay." The two of us shared a look, each one daring the other to be the first one to deface school property. Mind you, we had defaced a lot of property in one way or another, but this was right out in the open. There would be no denying what we had done if caught by one of the lifers.

I was younger and more ballsy back then, and I took my brush and painted half the brick. Jack had no choice but to finish the work. After he was done, being a perfectionist, I decided to add a second coat of paint to ensure that it looked good. We were careful, making sure that none of the burnt umber bled onto the mortar between the bricks. Time had stopped. So consumed were we by this moment, we didn't hear the pickup truck approaching down the driveway. Jack was the first to notice and exclaimed, "Someone's coming!" Mike Clancy, our boss, drove by, his arm hanging out the window and his seat set back to accommodate his big belly. With his dark glasses and his finely trimmed mustache, he looked directly at us, a wet paintbrush dangling by my side. Had we been caught? He waved and drove on, seemingly not noticing, or maybe he just didn't care. Jack and I looked at each other. He gave me his "Can you believe that?" look and I laughed. Then, we stepped back and admired the handiwork.

If you should find yourself in North Olmsted, Ohio with a few extra minutes, you can drive past the high school. There, if you know where to look, you'll find that brown brick, perfectly centered between two windows on the way to the soccer practice field at the back of the school. That brown brick is a testament to my love and friendship with Jack. It is a reminder of the people in my past who have left this earth, including my friend Jeff, who fought and supported me for many years. If you pause to admire the brick, listen hard enough and the echoed laughter of young men ready to take on the world will blow by you with a summer gush of wind.

Close your eyes and wait a little longer, and I'm sure you will hear the far-off strains of "Ana Ng" playing somewhere in the distance.

BIG AUDIO DYNAMITE
"RUSH"

I'm running through the streets of industrial Los Angeles cursing to myself. My eyes are searching, desperately scanning the sidewalk and disintegrating asphalt for a coat hanger. The sun beats down, and I'm sweating profusely. Behind me, my car is parked near the curb, the engine running and the keys locked inside it. Welcome to L.A., baby.

If there is a Horatio Alger rite-of-passage story in my life, it takes place during the summer of 1991. For three months, I worked as an intern for Alterian Studios, a special effects company in Hollywood. I was a 21-year-old kid — or at least I felt like a kid.

This feeling of being a child began as soon as I arrived in California. My mother and I spent three and a half days driving across the country in the 1987 Plymouth Horizon given to me that spring. The red, four-door hatchback was an automatic with crank windows, no AC, an FM/AM stereo and a little under a thousand miles on it. A great little car, it would be the perfect vehicle for navigating the L.A. freeways. It had been a good trip, with my mom and I having some thoughtful conversations. Upon arrival, though, she hovered over me protectively, as if I wouldn't survive in the big city. As much as I love her, I was relieved when she boarded the plane back to Ohio. This was my chance to be on my own. Although I would be living with my brother Budd and his fiancée, Karyn, in their apartment, they would be busy with their own lives and planning for their wedding for the following year. More often than not, I would be free to explore Los Angeles and figure out who I wanted to be.

This was a fine arrangement because Budd didn't know what to do with me. Although I was on the verge of being a college senior, he still viewed me as his pesky little brother, the dope who slammed a car door on his ankle, the kid who nicked up his drums and didn't tell him, the teenager he had to drive around on dates while I was on crutches in 9th grade. If Budd saw me that way, you can only imagine how his best friend, Tony Gardner, saw me. Tony is the genius responsible for the special effects in the remake of *The Blob* and *Darkman* (as well as future greats like *Army of Darkness, There's Something About Mary* and *Hairspray*). Alterian was his company and I must have looked like just another wide-eyed college dork when I walked through the doors of his shop for the first time.

My unpaid internship began as a runner. This meant that whatever supplies were needed, I was sent to pick them up in my little car. Simple, right? Not quite. In the age before Google Maps, all I had to work with was a massive map book called the Thomas Guide. It was thick with pages of city blocks broken into grids and an eye-straining index in the back with every street name of the greater Los Angeles area listed alphabetically. My first few weeks on the job were intense since I got lost numerous times. Luckily, I had music to steady my nerves. Before leaving Ohio, I had stuck Velcro to the dashboard of the Horizon and on the back of my black Emerson boombox. Voila! An instant dash-mounted cassette player. Yeah, it didn't work too well, but L.A. radio was still free of corporate influence and they played music that hadn't yet reached the Midwest. My station of choice was KROQ, spinning songs that formed the soundtrack to my Los Angeles summer: Dream Warriors' "My Definition of a Boombastic Jazz Style," Crowded House's "It's Only Natural," and Siouxie and the Banshees' "Kiss Them For Me," just to name a few.

No song revved me up more than Big Audio Dynamite's "Rush," which got cranked each time it came on the radio. Band leader Mick Jones' mash up of punky guitar power chords, hip-hop beats and a classic sample from the Who's "Baba O'Riley" make "Rush" one of the great anthems that cause you to want to bang your head and dance.

I worked as a runner without complaint for a month. I would have gone on that way for the remainder of the summer had it not been for the regular phone calls from my folks checking to ask what all I was learning on my internship. Here they were paying Bowling Green State University summer tuition so I could be in Los Angeles driving my car and doing grunt work for free. Their question started to fester in my head each afternoon when the heat began to rise and I invariably got stuck in the stop-and-go traffic on the freeways. I debated approaching Tony but fear gripped me whenever I was near him. Outside the shop he may have been a family friend, but within the walls of Alterian he was the *boss*. Couple that with the fact that I idolized the guy and dreamed of someday working with him as an equal, and whatever confidence I had when I started at Alterian disappeared.

Everything came to a head the day I locked my keys in the damn car with the engine running.

On this particular afternoon, lost in a sketchy, inner city neighborhood, I decided to ask for directions from a nearby parking lot attendant. Hurrying because I wanted to beat rush hour traffic on the dreaded 210 Freeway, I jumped out, locked my door and took off running. It only took two steps before I realized what I had done.

This leads us back to me jogging around, looking for a coat hanger to unlock my door. The only word coming out of my mouth was "fuck." Each time it had a different context: F- *"I'm such an idiot! What if my car gets stolen?"* U- *"I'm never going to make it back to the shop and I'm going to get fired!"* C- *"This isn't what I signed up for. What exactly am I learning?"* K- *"How is it possible that on the streets of L.A. I can't find a damn wire hanger? I know if I was in downtown Bowling Green I would probably find at least three within the first minute out of my car!"* Finally, I found a parking lot attendant with a slim jim tool and he took pity on me.

I completed my errand and stewed in my car the entire ride back to the shop. After unloading the supplies and turning in my receipts, I grew a spine and sat down with Tony. I laid it all out. I needed to learn. I wanted to contribute. I understood that supply runs and prepping the conference room for movie executives was part of the job, but I had more to offer. Since I was using the experience as a college credit, I had to have something to relay back to my advisor besides "I know how to make it to Burbank and back in under an hour." To my amazement, Tony agreed. He revised my schedule so that I would work with the artists during the afternoons.

The next day I was assigned to help paint the mechanical clock from *The Addams Family* movie. Full of pride, I left the shop feeling renewed, happily driving home with the window down and the radio at full blast. On that day, my summer kicked into high gear, my education just beginning.

BILLY JOEL
"AND SO IT GOES"

Maybe it's the fall or the fact that I'm *missing* the fall, but every September my heart starts to feel the season change as if it were turning from blood red to golden orange and yellow, like the trees I recall from my youth.

During these months, I can't help but think of my close friend Bob. Ours is a friendship that's grown into one of the tightest relationships I have. I was the best man in his first wedding, an honor I still hold close to my heart, even though that relationship didn't last. That wedding took place in late summer 1991, just after I returned from my California internship.

Bob and I met during my freshman year at Bowling Green; he was the pledge trainer in my fraternity. Since it was the band fraternity, I didn't take the organization too seriously. I was a cocky freshman who thought he was much better than those other band geeks. Thankfully, I learned what an ass I was, as the men in that fraternity became my best friends. Bob was there for my irrational tirade at my dorm mates over the death of Roy Orbison ("They just don't understand, man!"), my shock after being betrayed by a fraternity brother ("Fuckin' A, man!") and the driver of a cross-state road trip that found the two of us singing "Love Shack" by the B-52's and Tom Petty's "Free Fallin'."

The first semester of my sophomore year, Bob and I lived next door to each other in our dorm. That was the point when things changed in our friendship. Where we were once just a pledge trainer and a smartass freshman, Bob and I began turning to each other for advice, encouragement, and a mug of beer to cry into. Our time as neighbors was short-lived, though, as Bob left BG for an internship during his final semester of college. However, the die was cast, and our friendship grew stronger. Friendship requires work, especially when separated by miles. Bob never let the distance between us hinder our bond. He took the concept of brotherhood seriously and became another big brother to me.

For the remainder of my college years, whenever Bob came to Bowling Green for a visit, he was sure to stop by our house to hang out, maybe even crash for the night. On one of those visits, he proposed to his girlfriend in the stadium seats while a BG football game took place on the field down below. It was a great romantic gesture, one that's as clear to me today as the heat coming from the sun on that afternoon. Soon thereafter, he asked me to be his best man, and honestly, I had no clue what I was supposed to do.

Nevertheless, I stood by his side and watched as vows were exchanged. When Bob and his wife moved into their first apartment, I was a frequent visitor and considered it a safe haven away from home.

Sadly, the marriage didn't last. I feared for Bob and what the divorce would do to him. Would he be incredibly pissed? Would he be sad beyond consolation? I wasn't sure. To make matters worse, when his marriage ended, Julie and I were already living in California, so the best I could do was be a voice on the other end of the telephone. I felt helpless. And yet, Bob pulled through okay. He would fall in love again, he would accomplish great things in his life, and he would continue to be a stand-up guy. Each time we return to Cleveland, I make a point to call on my old friend. Even if we can only meet for lunch, it's worth the effort.

In my office hangs a black-and-white photograph of a waterfall that Bob took at Yosemite. I find the image profound and melancholy, and it reminds me of the fall season. When I stare at it long enough, I begin to hear the piano melody from "And So It Goes," the closing song from Billy Joel's album *Storm Front.* I've never been passionate about Joel's music, but that song, together with that waterfall, conjures up images of Bob's strength against the punches life has thrown at him. It could be the fact that I'm missing the fall or that I'm missing the blood red, golden orange and yellow leaves on the trees from my youth. But the truth is, I'm missing my friend and wishing the best for him.

INDIGO GIRLS
"GALILEO"

My bags sat on the floor waiting to be unpacked as I looked around my bedroom — the same bedroom where I'd grown up, the same bedroom I'd escaped when I went off to Bowling Green State University, and the same bedroom I would now live in as a college graduate trying to save up money to move to California. Nothing had changed in fifteen years. Not the wallpaper that my mother had hung, nor the newspaper clippings and magazine pictures tacked to the wall, nor the clown portrait hovering over the bunk beds, still unable to smile. A breeze came through the open window, bringing with it the smell of fresh cut grass. I felt lost. Four years of momentum seemed to have stalled while I waited out the summer. To top things off, an ill attempt to become a blond had left my hair orange.

Change was in the air, though. 1992 was an election year, and a youthful governor from Arkansas had begun to inspire twenty-somethings like me. We believed that our voices really could affect the outcome in November and help shape the country for years to come. In the music world, modern rock radio stations began popping up all over the country. Alternative became the mainstream. Exactly what "alternative" meant was up in the air, giving stations the freedom to play anything that didn't fit the mold of Top 40, country or classic rock radio. In Cleveland, it was WENZ, whose playlists were a collage of grunge, modern rock, folk, a little electronica and some of the great '80s college bands finally getting their due. During any hour you might hear the Replacements, Melissa Etheridge, Midnight Oil, Shawn Colvin and Pearl Jam. It was a healthy mix. One group I was pleased to receive wider exposure was Indigo Girls, who had just released their fourth album, *Rites of Passage.*

Amy Ray and Emily Saliers, the Indigo Girls, held a special place in my college experience. Jack and I spent the summer of '89 lounging on school rooftops or scaffoldings (when we should have been working) listening to their self-titled major-label debut. Their follow up, *Nomads, Indians, Saints*, found its way into my CD collection after a drunken night with my cousin Dave in 1991. It was eventually returned to his roommate but not before it had travelled to California and back. In '92, the newest single by Indigo Girls, "Galileo," was getting consistent airplay from WENZ. Saliers' introspective lyrics took me back to the many late-night conversations I had with Jack or Matt trying to figure out our place in the world. Hearing the perfect harmonies of the Indigo Girls had me believing that things would soon change.

But first, I needed a job.

At my mother's insistence, I interviewed with a local temp agency. One of her friends' sons had been quite successful in the temp world while he pursued his music career. It was worth a try. Dressed in my only pair of khakis and a faded dress shirt, I sat through an interview that was stifling and very corporate. It was the last thing I wanted to be doing with a film degree. After the interview, I returned home, collar unbuttoned, sleeves rolled up and slouched in a kitchen chair. My mood was grim and I was in need of a pick-me-up. A sudden urge compelled me to ring up my friend Sally, one of my few high school pals still living in the area. For months, I'd owed her a call. Perhaps a night out at one of North Olmsted's several dive bars would help lift my spirits. When she picked up after a few rings, she was her usual exuberant self.

"You're lucky you caught me," she stated. "I was on my way out the door to housesit for a friend all summer."

If I hadn't called her at that moment, I would have missed her all summer. Fate, perhaps? As we got caught up with each other's lives, I lamented about my job situation. Sally exclaimed, "You should come work with me!" She was working for a nonprofit organization called Cornucopia, Inc. Their staff taught mentally and physically handicapped adults basic job skills, such as proper etiquette and how to arrive at work on time, all in the setting of a natural food store. Cornucopia ran two such locations in Lakewood, a city twenty minutes east of where I lived: a grocery store called Nature's Bin and a small storefront fruit and vegetable market called simply, The Bin. It was meaningful work and I could help people while still busting my butt and earning the money I needed for California. It sounded perfect.

Sally set up an interview, and I was hired to train clients and work in the Nature's Bin grocery department. However, the night before my first day on the job, I was told instead to report to the smaller store, The Bin. I didn't know it then, but Fate was pulling strings again, and my life was about to change.

I rose at 6 a.m. to be to work by 6:45. My responsibilities included opening the store each morning. My manager was Barb, a large, friendly woman who shuffled through the store and stayed close to the register. My co-workers included Sally's boyfriend (and future husband), John, who was great to talk to about baseball; Cathy, a spirited young woman had some outrageous stories to share each day; and Stacey, John's brother-in-law. Stacey was the produce manager for both stores and stopped by regularly. His gruff, tough love demeanor made me laugh because he was a hell of a nice guy.

I set up crates and created fruit displays for foot traffic on the local sidewalk. I organized the cooler and kept the fruit and vegetable bins fully stocked and rotated. Best of all, I met some remarkable people, our clients, who were learning how to become citizens in the community. The work I did at The Bin felt useful —

worthwhile. The atmosphere at The Bin was generally relaxed, with a radio always on in the background, usually tuned to WENZ. I heard "Galileo" two or three times a day, and it never got old. The customers were all regulars, friendly locals who knew everyone by name. There was never a dull moment.

As I said, my life changed at that small store, most importantly my first Wednesday on the job. That day, one of the part-time employees came in for her regular Wednesday shift, a beautiful, curly-haired woman with enormous blue eyes and a smile to die for. Some people believe that soulmates are two souls split apart, searching for each other over lifetimes, sometimes reincarnated until they find each other. If that is true, then my soul finally got it right and found its other half the moment these words were spoken:

"Scott, this is Julie."

ROBBIE ROBERTSON
"WHAT ABOUT NOW"

I had a plan.

Having moved back in with my parents and taken a new job, I was determined to stay focused on moving to Los Angeles. I'd also just come out of a two-year relationship, wounded but thankful that it had ended, and I didn't believe I was ready to date. I thought it might be a distraction. So I had a plan to stay single.

Besides the hours I worked at The Bin, I spent most of my free time holed up in my parents' basement, catching up on movies I'd missed in the theater or listening to CD's on my new stereo. What I loved about that stereo unit was the six-CD changer with a shuffle feature. All I had to do was insert six compact discs, press "shuffle," and I had an instant jukebox. My compact disc collection wasn't too large back then, so my options were limited. Receiving heavy rotation at the time were *Woodface* by Crowded House, U2's masterpiece *Achtung Baby,* Springsteen's double shot from that year, *Human Touch* and *Lucky Town,* and Robbie Robertson's *Storyville.*

That last album, released in the fall of 1991, seemed destined to become a classic, especially after the glowing review it received by *Rolling Stone.* I got it based on the song "What About Now," which received modest airplay on Toledo's AOR station, WIOT. I was initially drawn to the haunting melody, but soon the lyrics grabbed me.

There's gonna be a change of season
Indian summer look around and it's gone
Why you wanna save the best for last
We grow up so slowly and grow old so fast

We don't talk about forever
We just catch it while we can
And if I grab on to the moment
Don't let it slip away out of my hand

I can't tell you how many times those words got me through my stressful final semester at college. The chorus, which features the harmonies of Robertson, Ivan Neville and the ethereal voice of Aaron Neville, echoed the lesson I took from my AP English class with Mr. Denman: carpe diem.

What about now
Forget about tomorrow
It's too far away

What about now

Close your eyes

Don't talk of yesterday

It's too far away, too far away

What about now

Storyville never became a classic. It was released a week after Nirvana's *Nevermind*, and we all know what happened after that. But I loved the album, especially that song.

As June rolled in, I made one final trip to visit Matt at Ohio University before he graduated. My excitement over the possibility of a lost weekend was dampened the Friday before I left. My mom called The Bin with the news that my dad was admitted to the hospital after a visit to his doctor. There was concern that something was wrong with his heart. A ripple of fear rushed through me. My family has a history of heart problems, and my father had been under a great deal of stress since the passing of my grandfather earlier in the year (plus, you know, a son graduating college, a daughter in summer school and the other son getting married). Both of my parents insisted that I keep my plans to visit Matt. A heart catheterization was scheduled for the following Monday, so there would be nothing to do but sit around and stare at the hospital walls for two days.

I drove down to Athens, Ohio, home to Ohio University. Soon after my arrival, my hardline stance against dating began to soften. As it would happen, my friend Sally was also in Athens that weekend. Matt and I met up with her at one of the local greasy spoons. We ate together, laughing and reminiscing about our high school days and the past four years. At one point, Sally asked me about my love life. I told her my plan, and she shook her head.

"What you need," she said, "is to date someone nice, like that Julie Flynn."

I was taken aback. Julie, the girl from The Bin?

Sally continued by saying how wonderful a person Julie was and that if I asked her out she would most surely say "yes." Sally might have also told me that Julie thought I was cute, but that may be my ego imagining it. We parted ways with Sally and her friends, and I spent the rest of the weekend destroying brain cells. But the seed was planted, and I left Athens thinking that maybe I *would* ask out that Julie Flynn. What harm could come from a couple of friendly dates? It's not like I was going to get serious.

Any plans of asking her out were tabled upon my arrival home. My dad needed to have life-saving quintuple bypass surgery. My mind froze. For the first time in my life, I worried about the mortality of my parents. Before, during, and after his operation, I used my job as a way to suppress my anger and fear. At the time, I was also the only child at home, so I tried to remain strong for my mom. I had never seen her so scared in my life.

"What am I going to do if I lose your father?" she cried.

Throughout my life, I'd only seen my mother and father as parents; I'd never comprehended them as husband and wife who loved each other until death do they part.

Thankfully, my father's staggering surgery was a success. The recovery was slow, though. As he regained his strength, his restored heart filled him with vigor. Both my mom and dad became, dare I say, feisty, like newlyweds. It was quite a sight. In many ways, "What About Now" could have been my dad's anthem. From this experience, I had a new respect of the aspect of love and keeping my heart open in case the right person came along.

In mid-July, Budd married Karyn in California. After the wedding, my folks went to Hawaii for a well-deserved vacation. This left my younger sister, Heidi, and me home alone. I was forced to confront a lot of the shit I'd been suppressing for a couple of months. Luckily Matt was there, waiting with a twelve pack of Pabst Blue Ribbon and a stack of CDs. For one week straight, the two of us adjourned to the basement each night after I got off work.

As the sun set and the basement grew darker, the two of us would sit downstairs in decrepit old yellow rocking chairs, smoking, drinking and listening to music, the CD changer mystically choosing the songs that fit our mood. With the memories of my brother's wedding fresh in my mind, I looked inward and wondered if I would be alone the rest of my life. Thinking about my parents and their brush with death, I openly wept in the darkness of the smoke-filled room. Meanwhile, "What About Now" played through the stereo.

"Why aren't you dating right now?" Matt asked.

"Because I've decided not to see anyone until I move to L.A. I want to stay focused."

There was a long pause as he rolled a cigarette, lit it up and took a long drag. Once the orange glow had faded away, Matt spoke. Smoke seeped out of the corner of his mouth.

"Dude, that is the stupidest fucking thing I've ever heard."

We doubled over with laughter. He was so on the mark. By placing a self-imposed restriction on dating, I was denying myself the chance to find happiness.

"What about now?" Robertson sang.

"What *about* now?" I thought.

In that moment, I decided to ask Julie out the next time I saw her. I would soon discover that my future had been working alongside me all along.

BRUCE SPRINGSTEEN
"BOOK OF DREAMS"

It was the last Wednesday of July, and Julie was working the cash register of The Bin. The store was empty when I hurried in through the side door and looked her way, having just mustered up my courage in the alley outside. With half a store of fruits and vegetables between us, I fumbled through asking her on a date.

"So, uh, if you're not doing anything this weekend, I was wondering if maybe, uh, you'd want to go to a movie or something?"

She smiled excitedly and said, "Yes."

"Cool," I replied, then quickly returned to the alley and pumped my fist in triumph.

It was going to be like any other first date: go to a movie, go for a bite to eat afterwards, get to know each other, and, if lucky enough, share a goodnight kiss. Just a fun night out with the pretty co-worker whose smile warmed the dark corners of The Bin. I wasn't looking for a relationship. I certainly wasn't looking for love.

But that's what I found on Saturday, August 1, 1992, when Julie Flynn and I went on our first date.

Julie suggested we go see the movie *Unlawful Entry*, a thriller starring Kurt Russell, Madeleine Stowe and Ray Liotta. She picked me up in her Volkswagon Fox and we drove to the Great Northern movie theater in the heart of North Olmsted. *Unlawful Entry* was an average film, never rising above being a 'B' movie. To this day, I'm surprised that Julie chose this film. Thrillers, especially ones about stalkers, are the kind of movies she hates. However, she seemed to enjoy it back then. With the night still young, we drove to Frank's Place, one of several dark, smoke-filled watering holes in North Olmsted. Frank's Place is notable because it is located in a plaza directly under the North Olmsted water tower, right next door to the convenience store where Matt and I shoplifted that stack of comics when we were kids.

We talked over a couple of beers, slowly stripping away some of our guarded layers and revealing parts of ourselves. Hunger struck so we drove to Arturo's, another bar, though this one with a kitchen. While I picked my way through an order of chicken wings, our conversation continued.

What we talked about wasn't deep. We didn't discuss politics or the depth of the film we just saw (because there wasn't really any), but I was affected by the ease with which we were able to open up to each other. I could have told her anything, and I knew she wouldn't judge me. Everything felt so natural, like I'd known her my entire life. I remember thinking, "This girl is special." I also thought, "Man, I want to kiss her."

The evening came to an end and Julie drove me home. When she parked in the driveway I wanted to kiss her, but I didn't want to be presumptuous. So, for only the second time in my life, I asked a girl if I could kiss her.

"May I kiss you?"

"I'd like that."

Our lips met. A thunderbolt crashed down from the heavens and opened up my heart. I don't know the duration of that first kiss in actual time, but in a grand sense it has lasted twenty years.

We said goodnight but not before I asked when I could see her again.

"Tomorrow," she replied.

I left her car and floated into the house a changed man. My sister saw me enter in my blissful daze.

"What's up with you?" Heidi asked.

"I think I just went out with the woman I'm going to marry."

I saw Julie the next day and every day after that for the rest of my life.

Three weeks into our bliss, I did the obvious thing and made her a mix tape. Cut me a little slack: I'd just bought a new stereo, a new toy. Pouring through my LP's, cassettes and CD's, I did my best to combine songs that she liked, songs I thought she'd like and songs from my heart, all on a Maxell UR90.

"Hey, Hey Julie" was a collection of pop, rock and Broadway songs that included the B-52's, Poi Dog Pondering, Bonnie Raitt with Was (Not Was) and Barbra Streisand. I even got creative and had James Newton Howard's fanfare from the movie *Grand Canyon* segue into "Learning to Fly" by Tom Petty and the Heartbreakers. Knowing I'd have to include my favorite artist, Bruce Springsteen, I chose "Book of Dreams" from his 1992 release, *Lucky Town*. The song is simple and direct, a sparse acoustic love song to his wife, Patti Scialfa. It describes a wedding day and the mystery and wonder that awaits the lovers after they exchange their vows. The lyrics spoke everything about how I felt for Julie. When I gave her the mix tape, I pointed out "Book of Dreams" for her to listen to closely, as if to say, "This is how I feel."

The next month was full of our own mystery and wonder. Falling in love so quickly raised hundreds of questions. I did some heavy soul searching, each time thinking, "How is this possible?" My heart would counter with, "Search yourself and you'll realize that she's your soulmate." I recalled the series of events that brought me to this moment: the chance phone call with my friend Sally that led to my job; the unexpected move to working at The Bin that happened the night before I was to start the job; how it seemed so right that I ask Julie out despite my plans for the future; and, of course, the thunderbolt that hit me when we kissed for the first time.

Being with Julie was what I wanted deep in my soul. I concluded that sometimes the stars align and you're given the gift of a lifetime.

You're not supposed to question the universe.

When I told Julie how I felt, I was amazed to learn that she felt the same way. Wherever I was going to go in life, she wanted to be with me on that journey.

As the summer came to an end, Julie and I began discussing getting married. I secretly began saving for an engagement ring and learned how to play the guitar. Julie had mentioned that she once wished someone would propose to her by singing Firefall's "You Are the Woman." I thought I'd make her wish become a reality. Approaching Matt to teach me how to play the song on the acoustic guitar, my old friend, in his infinite wisdom, put the kibosh on Firefall.

"Scott," he said, "isn't there something more personal you could play for her other than this 1970s soft rock fluff?"

I didn't have to think twice about it.

For two months, I practiced the basic chords Matt showed me, planning on a Christmastime proposal. But it was not meant to happen that way. Over the Thanksgiving holiday, my parents held an east coast wedding reception for Budd and Karyn. With the entire family under one roof, my new sister-in-law suggested that I propose that weekend because Julie would never expect it.

The night of the party, I led Julie down to the basement so we could have some privacy. I sat her down, whipped out Matt's guitar and sang her "Book of Dreams." At first she didn't realize what was going on. As soon as I dropped to my knee and produced the ring, she figured it out.

Needless to say, she said, "Yes!"

Twenty years ago, I went on a date that changed my life. The movie wasn't memorable and the food afterwards was bland. But the conversation and that kiss…oh man, that kiss rocked my world. Twenty years later, Julie and I have our own book of dreams and new chapters are being written every day.

POSITION
IEC TYPE I • NORMAL

maxell UR 90

UR 90 HEY, HEY, JULIE! maxell

A DATE . .
N.R. ○YES ○NO

Dreamland - B-52's
Baby Mine - Bonnie Raitt and Was (Not Was)
Too Much Passion - Smithereens
The Angels - Melissa Etheridge
Shining Star - INXS
UNTIL The END of the World - U2
GRAND CANYON FANFARE
Learning To Fly - Tom Petty & The Heartbreakers
Kid Fears - Indigo Girls
Recurring Dream - Crowded House
Within Your Reach - The Replacements

B DATE . .
N.R. ○YES ○NO

Proud Mary - Ike & Tina Turner
The Ballad of Peter Pumpkinhead - XTC.
Book Of Dreams - Bruce Springsteen
What I Am - Edie Brikell and New Bohemians
Be The One - Poi Dog Pondering
Wild Night - Martha Reeves
Bring Him Home - from LES MISÉRABLES
Getting To Know You - James Taylor
Left Of Center - Suzanne Vega
All This Time - Sting
Send In The Clowns - Barbara Streisand

A HEY, HEY, JULIE! **B** FROM SCOTT, AUG '92

JULIE, I HOPE YOU CAN GET INTO THESE TUNES. I TRIED TO MIX IT UP. LOVE, SCOTT

TOM PETTY & THE HEARTBREAKERS
"SOUTHERN ACCENTS"

On December 26, 1993, Jack and I hung out in the Malchus basement for the last time. Four days before my wedding, this would be our last opportunity to just "be," having a few drinks and listening to music. After the wedding, Jack would return to the south and I would move west with my new bride. It had been the plan that the two of us would hang out for the night instead of heading to some bar or trying to organize a small party.

Our evening began with throwing back 7 & 7's and watching *Falling Down*, starring Michael Douglas, on the TV set up in the far corner of the basement. If we had gauged the evening on the quality of *Falling Down*, I wouldn't be writing this. Or, perhaps *because* of the letdown of the film, I am writing this. You see, after the movie there wasn't much to say. Even two or three drinks couldn't erase the disappointment we both felt. Eschewing an intellectual discussion about the plight of the middle-class, white-collar working man, we agreed that the movie was a piece of crap and turned instead to an old reliable: the music. I threw on *Southern Accents,* the 1986 album by Tom Petty & the Heartbreakers, and we discussed the wedding, the move, Jack's relationship with his girlfriend. Bullshit, really. But the good kind of bullshit, the kind of bullshit upon which friendships are built. It's like the conversations in the film *Diner*: comfort talk.

"Don't Come Around Here No More" began playing. This song has always had a special meaning to the two of us. In 1987, the year Jack's graduated high school, we went to a Tom Petty & the Heartbreakers concert at Blossom Music Center. It was the ultimate summer show (the Georgia Satellites and the Del Fuegos both opened). In the weeks leading up to the show, we'd drive around town in the Whomobile, waiting for a Petty song to come on. Even though the song was a couple of years old at the time, "Don't Come Around Here No More" was still a favorite by the local DJ's. Every time the song played while I was driving, the two of us would pound the crap out of the crumbling vinyl dashboard of the Delta 88. It's one of my lasting memories of that old car: Jack and I beating on that dash, thrashing back and forth in the front seat while the crescendo of the song blasted over the car speakers.

With that memory in mind, I jumped up, grabbed some old cassette (I like to think it was my copy of *Anderson Bruford Wakeman Howe,* since Jack openly mocked the group) and placed tape over the tabs. We were going to make a compilation. I started the Petty song over and announced my ingenious plan. The two of us would make the mix tape together, each of us alternating songs. My music collection may have been limited at the time, but that wasn't important. We could certainly fill 100 minutes of music from what I owned. My plan may have been to commemorate our friendship or create a lasting collection of music we could always look back on, but Jack had other things in mind. He chose to think thematically about the occasion and picked several songs that spoke about our lives at that point in time. Thus, we created a collection that not only traveled down the nostalgia highway but took its place in line of the important moments in our lives.

The road map of our friendship is laid out on that tape. "Rock Lobster" shows up, but it's cut short because we both got sick of the song after its fifth minute. Years later I would realize that we shut the tape off literally thirty seconds before the song ended. Still, when you've had enough, you must end the madness. Simple Minds, Springsteen, the Who, Van Halen and the Outfield weave into the mix from our years in high school. They Might Be Giants, the Smithereens, Joe Jackson, the Reivers and Springsteen (again) parade around from our college years. All of these songs have a special meaning to us, even ""Bust A Move" by Young MC. However, the other songs Jack chose, the songs that were thematically linked to that night, are ones that I return to time and again. "The Road Not Taken" by Bruce Hornsby and the Range was Jack's way of saying "good luck" and that he was proud of me following my dream. "Independence Day" by Bruce was Jack speaking about the two of us growing up in the Cleveland suburbs, doing everything we could to get out of Ohio and become our own men. And "Athena" by the Who…well, okay, I have no idea why he put that one on. It was the end of the night and there was only room for one more song. After 5 or 6 drinks, you go with what thrills you in the minute.

The one song that sticks to me from all of the selections that night was the second one recorded. And we didn't even lift the record needle. Once "Don't Come Around Here No More" ends, the lovely title track closes out side one of the album.

"I love this song. Let it play," Jack said. It was his selection, I thought, so he can pick what he wants. Looking back, I'm glad he chose it.

"Southern Accents" is quite simply one of the most beautiful songs that Petty has ever written. Quiet and restrained, it really captures the blue collar/southern experience theme that he was trying to achieve throughout the entire album. Benmont Tench's piano is practically the sole instrument, with very light accompaniment by the great Stan Lynch on drums. Mike Campbell has a brief moment on the dobro, and Howie Epstein's angelic harmony vocals shine elsewhere. Finally, the legendary Jack Nitzche created a string arrangement that gives the piece a greater sense of heartache and power.

If you are only familiar with Petty's hits, you must go back and listen to "Southern Accents." Petty's prayer to the South, lost love, and his mother (who had passed away shortly before the recording of the album) is sure to move you. It invokes a sense of place so vividly that when I hear it I recall my relatives who live in Alabama. They do things their own way and take pride in who they are and their southern heritage. With so much history in the South, I'm sure that's one of the reasons Jack chose to live there (besides basketball and the good woman who would become his wife).

At certain moments, Petty may be speaking to the ghost of his mother and imagining her there alongside him. However, like so many classic works of art, Petty leaves just enough ambiguity for his audience to insert themselves into the story. In my youth, unaware of the circumstances under which Petty wrote "Southern Accents," I imagined the song was about a woman he loved and had lost.

How many of us have had "the One" slip away? You thought he or she would change your life for the better, but in the end you suffered a broken heart. If you're lucky, your true love is waiting around the corner to help mend those gaping wounds. If you're not so lucky, as some of my dear friends have not been, you wind up at the bottom of a bottle, consumed with despair. Jack and I had been through so much in our lives when this song got laid to tape. We had seen each other at our worst and had been there for each other in those times of need. I don't think Jack intended "Southern Accents" to serve as a reminder of our past and the closing of this chapter in our lives, but it turned out to be the perfect song for that moment, the perfect song for "The Final Basement Tape."

I have listened to my copy of that tape (Jack has the original) hundreds of times since December 26, 1993. I'm always amazed at how well the songs flow together. The two of us were literally running around the house, tracking down songs, trying to keep the other one in the dark to ensure that the next one was an unexpected surprise. After Julie and I moved, my tape wound up in the car where it would sit for months at a time. When I was feeling low, it would mystically drop out of the glovebox, and I would play it for weeks on end. I've never grown tired of those songs, not even Mellencamp's "Pop Singer." Then the tape would be put away until the next time I was seeking the comfort of an old friend.

Several winters ago, I pulled it out while I took down the Christmas lights. Like a fool, I chose my old black boombox, long retired and notorious for ruining cassettes. It ate the tape, of course, destroying my copy forever. Luckily, I had found digital versions of the songs and burned a CD. But honestly, it's not the same. The imperfections of my LP's are missing. And the terrible hisses from my warped cassettes, some of them second-generation recordings, are also missing. There was something pure about that original tape, like my friendship with Jack.

Each and every time I hear "Southern Accents," I'm back in the basement on that December night. It's frigid cold outside and the two of us are just sitting there, taking in the music, nodding to one another with slight smiles on our faces. Our lives are about to head down a new road. I'm going to get married and move away and there won't be any more nights like this (I was wrong about that one).

In one sense, "Southern Accents" could be considered the last true basement song of my life. It is the final good memory I have of my parents' old house and the fortress of solitude where I learned so much about myself. Thankfully, it was not the last time I would see Jack. Our friendship since that night has grown and we've become closer. I trust him more than anyone other than Julie and my family. I would trust him with my children in a heartbeat. That is how much of a brother Jack is to me.

I dream of a day when we may live closer to each other, of his children knowing mine. I dream of a lot of things. But until that day comes, I still have "Southern Accents" to soothe me and get me through to the next day.

LOS LOBOS
"BE STILL"

Cleveland in the wintertime can be a cruel, desolate town. The wind chill often drops below zero, and gray slush mounds crowd the streets, seeping onto the asphalt, creating black ice. The skies are barren of clouds, yet the sun's rays can't seem to warm you from a cold so biting that no matter how many layers you wear, shaking the chill from your bones is near impossible. When you're outside, if your nostrils don't stick together, your breath hangs in the air as if you've exhaled a small cloud. You have no choice in where you grow up, and since Cleveland is the community where Julie and I were born and raised, we were destined to have our wedding there.

On December 30th, 1993, our friends and family from all over the country braved inclement weather to witness Julie and I exchange our vows. St. Malachi's in downtown Cleveland was still decorated with Christmas poinsettias, and the lights were dimmed as guests entered the old, welcoming church. Although one of our friends was mugged on the way there and a couple of the tuxes didn't match the rest of the groom's party, the ceremony went off without any real hitches. By the time I saw Julie walking down the aisle with her father, nothing else mattered. After the moment her hand joined mine at the altar, I had a perpetual smile on my face for the remainder of the night. There was a brief thought in which I questioned whether I should be more nervous, but it was fleeting. I was too damn elated. Even though our courtship had been fast (we were engaged just four months after our first date) and some questioned whether we knew what we doing, my soul had been fulfilled the instant Julie and I kissed for the first time. Marrying her was the surest decision I've ever made in my life.

After the ceremony and the wedding photos, we adjourned to nearby St. Mary's Church for the reception. By the time Julie and I had arrived at the banquet hall, most of my cousins had begun drinking shots to commemorate our union (I may have had one, too). Our two hundred guests enjoyed an excellent meal (of which I think I had two bites) while we went table to table to greet everyone who had gathered in our honor. To save costs, a videographer wasn't hired, but my sister-in-law, Karyn, walked around with her own video camera and recorded various comments from people. This worked out wonderfully even *after* she'd had a few too many and the footage started to resemble Woody Allen's *Husbands and Wives.* Near the end of the tape, Karyn began a conversation with someone and forgot to shut off the camera while it hung at her side, capturing about ten minutes of her talking while you only see the floor. This may be one of my favorite moments of the entire recording.

We hired this dude, Rick O'Bannion, a local radio disc jockey who did weddings on the weekends, to spin music that night. I call him "dude" because Rick was a throwback to the '80s music scene: long hair, a bushy 'stache, tinted glasses, tight jeans and weathered cowboy boots. He looked every bit as gravelly as his smoky radio voice.

Beforehand, we had laid out our ground rules: no chicken dance, no hokey pokey, no Kenny G and *absolutely* no Celine Dion. We provided Rick with the three songs that made up our wedding dance set. The first, "Book of Dreams" by Bruce Springsteen, was the love song I learned to strum on guitar in order to propose to Julie. The second was a ballad by acclaimed jazz singer Diane Schurr. Rounding out the selections was a lovely Los Lobos song from their album *The Neighborhood,* "Be Still."

Written by songwriters David Hidalgo and Louis Perez, this isn't a typical wedding dance number. If memory serves, most of us had some trouble moving in time to the 6/8 rhythm. Yet, it's a song of hope. Like a parent who bids his or her child adieu as their car drives off to a new town, "Be Still" encourages the progression of life while carrying a touch of melancholy as it reflects on the past.

Before the celebration began in earnest: guests dancing or pouring more drinks down their throats, the sharing of old stories of when Julie and I were kids, a groomsman spending the night with his face in a toilet, one of my friends grabbing *his* brother by the throat, the booze running out, the never-ending taking of family pictures, my brother-in-law wearing Julie's veil, my cousin and brother dragging me on my back across the grimy floor...before all of that could happen, it was important that not just Julie and I, but all of us, were anointed by the exquisite lyrics of Hidalgo and Perez.

Outside St. Mary's, unaccommodating weather made life miserable for anyone unfortunate enough to be stuck at a bus stop or driving the icy roads. Inside the church, though, the good spirits and warmth of love was felt as two families merged to create vivid memories that will last my lifetime. Still, none of those memories would mean much if not for Julie, my wife, my best friend, my soulmate.

In 1993, "Be Still" was a blessing on the newlyweds as we embarked on uncharted territory. Through the years, I have given this song to friends and family as they have become new parents. After twenty years by Julie's side, I continue to believe that "Be Still" is the perfect melody to usher us out of every December and into January. With each anniversary and each new year, we gain a fresh start to better ourselves and become better people.

Here's hoping we all can stay gold and be still and that the calm blue waters wash our souls and that our hearts are one.

CROWDED HOUSE
"DISTANT SUN"

Julie sat on the floor of our new apartment, crying.

"We've just lost our only friends," she said.

Our move to California had been full of uncertainty. Julie and I were blessed to have my brother and his wife to help make the transition smoother, but after a month of living with them we knew the time had come to get a place of our own. We found an apartment that was close to their house and cheap, everything you could ask for as strangers in a new city.

The day of our move was long and our nerves were fried. We just wanted to get settled, but no matter how much we seemed to get done, there were still stacks of boxes in the living room, and the mound of suitcases thrown in a corner seemed to have slowly become a mountain.

It was on my last trip to Budd and Karyn's house to pick up some remaining items that I learned our bed had created dents in their hardwood floors. Karyn was livid, and I didn't know what to say. Julie and I thought we had been careful, that we had done everything we could to protect the floors. To end our stay with them on such a bad note felt horrible. It really did feel like we'd lost our only friends.

This wasn't how our new life was supposed to begin, in tears and guilt.

As Julie sat with her knees pressed against her chest, I did my best to comfort her and assure her that it would all be okay. A more clever man would have come up with better words, but I was exhausted, equally scared and frankly, not that clever.

For instance, I should have quoted from Neil Finn and the song he wrote for Crowded House, "Distant Sun." It's one of the most beautiful, tormented love songs I've ever heard. It was the band's first single from their fourth album, *Together Alone*, in 1993. Unfortunately, it received minimal recognition by radio programmers once grunge shook up the music industry. The first few times I heard the song, I swear I had to stop what I was doing and listen attentively.

Everything about "Distant Sun" is glorious: Neil Finn's aching vocals, Mark Hart's chiming twelve-string guitar, Nick Seymour's understated bass playing, and the late Paul Hester's great drumming and perfect vocal harmonies. Of all the song's strengths, it's the bridge and the twelve words that Finn cries leading into the guitar solo that fill me with the most emotion. In anguish, desperation, and with all of his heart, the singer confesses his inadequacy in easing his lover's pain. With nothing left to offer, he offers his heart.

He offers love.

In just twelve words, Finn transforms what was already one of the prettiest songs ever written into an instant classic. Has any phrase ever sung so plainly explained true love? In my life, there have been so many instances when Julie has been hurting and I haven't had an adequately soothing response. Whatever words I've come up have been useless. But as I learned from Crowded House song, I have something else to offer besides mere words: I have love.

Having Julie by my side made pursuing my dream of becoming a screenwriter achievable. It's humbling when I think of the sacrifice she made, uprooting herself from her family in Cleveland to embark on a journey with me, some schmo with big glasses and bad clothes (she would eventually help me remedy that). It wasn't easy for her and I'm not going to mince words: Julie *hated* Los Angeles. It didn't make life any easier that I was doing grunt work as a production assistant, which meant long hours and low pay. Being apart seemed to contradict the idea of taking on the world together.

Yet she never said, "Let's go back." To this day she's never told me, "You've given it your best shot, time to pack it in." Ever since I met her, Julie has been my strongest supporter. She has been my rock.

And so, being not clever, all I could do was wrap my arms around my teary-eyed wife in that long hallway between our bedroom and living room. Eventually we went to bed in our new home, only to be woken up the next morning by the class bells of nearby North Hollywood High. That day, everything would smooth over between Budd and Karyn, and they would grow to become our closest friends.

There would be many great adventures during our first year in L.A. – adopting our three cats (Otis, Ella and Doodle), the wonderful visit from Julie's sisters and friends, and the disastrous visit from Matt. There would also be more nights of tears by both of us, as we navigated our new lives together. Through heartache, confusion and anger, we figured out a way to make it, not as individuals, but as a couple…as Julie and Scott.

AL GREEN
"LET'S STAY TOGETHER"

Our second apartment was the coolest place that we've ever lived. That's not to say that our current house isn't cool. It's just that the one bedroom/loft apartment that Julie and I moved into in 1995 had an air about it that rang true of a young married couple laying down roots. Located on Moorpark St. in North Hollywood, it wasn't a large place, per se – a modest kitchen, a small balcony off the living room, an even larger balcony off the loft – but it had high ceilings and an openness about it that was very inviting.

Our first place had been located around the corner from North Hollywood High School. With a regular bell schedule and a busy street, it was not an ideal home. Add to that the lack of air conditioning during the 100+ degree summers and you might say we were justified in wanting a new apartment. The Moorpark complex where we moved to was quiet, backed up against a shady residential neighborhood and was within walking distance of shops and restaurants.

A quarter mile from our front door, located on the corner of Moorpark and Tujunga, was Henry's Tacos, a San Fernando landmark with great Mexican food. Across the street from Henry's, on the other corner of Tujunga, was a shopping plaza with a 7-Eleven, a laser disc rental store (which closed a year later) and Sushi 101, one of our favorite hangouts with Budd and Karyn.

If you walked south of Henry's, perhaps another three-hundred yards down Tujunga, you'd find another plaza that housed the Laundromat we used, some small boutique stores and a teriyaki stand that made some of the best chicken teriyaki you could find (pretty cheap, too). I wouldn't call the area we lived in trendy – our apartment was one in a row of buildings along Moorpark, but the side streets behind Moorpark did have some beautiful, expensive houses I would admire during morning jogs. I'd look at those homes and dream of the day when Jules and I would be able to afford our own house. Until then, I was content with our cool loft apartment.

During those years, Julie worked at a small flower shop in North Hollywood. The hours sucked, she worked almost every holiday, and the owners were assholes. I oscillated between Alterian Studios, the make-up effects company where I'd done my summer internship in '91, and a production company that turned out sing-along videos for children. Of the two jobs, I preferred Alterian, where I'd moved up from production assistant to coordinator. It was stressful but fulfilling. The other job was a paycheck, and even though I worked with good people I just never felt committed to them. I sense that they felt the same way about me.

In truth, I wasn't going to be satisfied with either job because my goal was to write and direct movies, a goal that the space in the loft provided me room to pursue. Despite the closeness to the living room, the loft felt separate from the rest of the apartment. No door closed it off from the downstairs, just a long staircase that led up to my creative zone. It was up there that I wrote *Southern Cross*, the screenplay that evolved into my film, *King's Highway.*

Whether is was a big dinner party in which the guests had plenty of space to socialize, or an intimate get together with close friends, the Moorpark apartment exuded hospitality. Many of our best memories came from spur-of-the-moment decisions to take in a meal at Sushi 101 with Budd and Karyn and return to the apartment with a six-pack and a bottle of wine.

One Saturday night in '96, the four of us were laughing and reminiscing, as couples do, when Karyn had the great idea for a lip-sync contest. It wasn't really a contest because Julie (to the best of my recollection; we were pretty loose that night) was the only one to "perform." Karyn chose Al Green's "Let's Stay Together" to begin the show. Julie went up the stairs while I started the music. As Reverend Green began to sing, Jules appeared over the railing, masterfully mouthing the words to the song. In perfect stride to the beat of the song, she walked down, step by step, until she was "on stage" in front of us.

Julie's years in high school show choir came out as she delivered a great performance, one that had us laughing and applauding. I couldn't keep my eyes off of her, my cheeks aching from the huge smile on my face. Watching her I had a longing in my heart to have known her back when she was a teenager. How I wish someone had videotaped her on stage in front of a real crowd. Julie has such a beautiful voice, but moreover, she commands your attention when the spotlight is on her. Even when merely lip-syncing a '70s soul staple like "Let's Stay Together," she's a star. It's a quality that she's passed down to both of our children.

My God, I was so in love with her in that moment. What had I done to deserve this funny, beautiful woman by my side, supporting my dreams, never once doubting me?

While our first hot, awful apartment was about getting established as a married couple in a new city, our second place and those next couple of years saw us setting down roots that proved we could survive whatever challenges life threw our way.

Notice of a rent increase came in mid-1997, around the same time Budd and Karyn became pregnant with their first child. Watching the two of them go through the trials and tribulations of becoming parents made Julie and I seriously evaluate our lives and priorities. We discussed when we would want our own children and whether the Moorpark apartment would be the right place to begin a family. Although we loved the area, we didn't think it was accommodating enough. So by September, we moved.

When I recall our first year together, it's a blur. So much happened that the first apartment felt like a weigh station in our marriage. The second place felt like our first home, as we had a comfort in that area that made us feel secure. Julie and I created lasting memories in that apartment and proved to ourselves that we were survivors.

This was a vital lesson for the years to come.

FLEETWOOD MAC
"LANDSLIDE"

Karyn and I sat mesmerized at the sight of Stevie Nicks and Lindsey Buckingham performing "Landslide." We weren't at the Greek Theater or one of L.A.'s other revered concert venues; we were sitting in her living room watching Fleetwood Mac's *The Dance*, the 1997 concert reunion of the band's classic lineup. Released on video the same year, I had received it as a Christmas gift from Budd and Karyn on a night Julie and I were over for dinner, just before we flew back to Cleveland for the holidays. With the video playing on their VCR, the Mac served as our background music throughout the night. While none of us really stopped to watch the concert, at one point Julie and Budd were in the kitchen and I found myself sitting next to Karyn. That's when "Landslide" began to play.

I've always liked Fleetwood Mac, my earliest exposure coming during their peak years when "Don't Stop," "Tusk" and "Sara" were staples of FM radio. "Gypsy," from their 1982 album, *Mirage*, has been one of my favorite songs since I first heard it. Buckingham's guitar solo at the end? Masterful. Following my freshman year of college, I really became a fan, thanks to Jack introducing me to *Rumours*, the band's monumental album from 1977. It was then that I learned the background of the group and how the five band mates – Buckingham, Nicks, Christine McVie, John McVie and Mick Fleetwood – managed to keep working together despite betrayals, broken hearts and a lot of drugs. When *The Dance* special premiered in mid '97, I was among the millions who were excited that Buckingham had returned to the fold a decade after leaving the band. Watching the five members interact with affection was remarkable, especially on Nicks' haunting ballad.

"Landslide" is a song that she premiered when she joined Fleetwood Mac in 1975. It was never released as a single back then, but it became a concert favorite and gained a beloved following throughout the years, even generating a moving cover by Smashing Pumpkins in 1994. For the duration of *The Dance*, Nicks and Buckingham, the ex-lovers whose turbulent past fueled many of the band's most poignant songs, stood center stage in the spotlight. This duet of just Nicks' aged voice and Buckingham's intricate guitar playing, both instruments performed with a passion often lacking in artists whose salad days are behind them, is the highlight of the concert. Besides the song, "The Chain," no song by Fleetwood Mac has gained more depth as the years have progressed. When Nicks sang "Landslide" at that concert, the soulfulness with which she performed had me believing that the reunion marked the beginning of a new chapter in her life. It was a sentiment I understood.

1997 had been full of many transitions for the Malchus families that the last few months didn't feel like the closing of just another calendar year but the end of a chapter in all of our lives. Julie was finishing up her college courses, we had moved into a new apartment, and most importantly, Budd and Karyn were expecting their first child in early 1998. It had been a long, emotional journey for them as they'd been trying to become parents for over a year.

Our nights of getting together on a whim would become few and far between, along with those Saturdays of drinking and listening to loud music and the occasional prank calls to relatives in different time zones (my apologies to my aunt and uncle in North Olmsted). We'd now have to consider how our actions would affect the life of a small child, something that took years to sink into my thick skull. Jules and I weren't a couple on the cusp of parenthood, but our relationship with Budd and Karyn was so close that when their lives changed, so did ours. Over the course of the year, they went through the highs and lows of trying to get pregnant and we were there with them, experiencing many of the same emotions. I was deeply moved by their perseverance and finally began to feel that I was up to the task of being a father myself.

That night, as we celebrated Christmas and the good fortune that 1998 promised, Karyn and I were entranced with the sight of the two rock-and-roll luminaries and the gorgeous sound of

"Landslide." When the song ended, I swear I saw a glimmer of tears in Karyn's eyes. She had wanted for so long to be a mother, and now she was just months away from becoming one.

"Everything's changing," she said in a quiet voice. "Nothing's going to be the same."

Once Budd and Karyn had their baby, nothing *would* be the same.

I couldn't wait.

BRYAN ADAMS
"(EVERYTHING I DO) I DO IT FOR YOU"

As my daughter Sophie begins to explore music, I hope she'll someday take a trip through the hundreds of LPs, cassettes and compact discs that Julie and I have amassed over the years. When she comes across a certain single, I imagine that her mouth will gape slightly, and those beautiful blue eyes of hers will roll as she says, "Seriously, Dad, Bryan Adams?" At that point, I'll sit Sophie down to recount the night she was born, explaining how Adams' "(Everything I Do) I Do It for You" became a part of our record collection. I'm sure it will go something like this…

Sophie,

We weren't supposed to be in the hospital on January 4, 1999, as your due date was later in the month. However, your mom was recovering from a twenty-four hour flu and her doctor had her admitted to replenish her fluids. Hospital policy dictated that your tiny heart rate be monitored as long as mom was a patient. To our surprise, your little heart was beating too fast, and we weren't allowed to check out until it slowed down. After several hours, nothing changed so the doctor decided it was time to deliver you. Labor was induced, and your mom spent a long night living through contractions, while all I could do was rub her back and talk her through the pain.

January 4th became the 5th, and you still were not with us. Complications arose in that early Tuesday afternoon, complications the doctor felt were very dangerous for both you and your mom so she was rushed to the operating room for a Cesarean section. Though I was afraid, I had complete confidence in the doctor. What kept me grounded was the knowledge that in a short while we would be holding you, and our life as a family would begin.

The rest of that day is a series of snapshots: The operation. The doctor lifting you into the world. Cutting the umbilical cord. Hearing you cry for the first time.

Your paternal grandparents arrived from Arizona, having left their house very early that morning. Your Uncle Mike (who lived in California at that time) floated around, giddy. Your Uncle Budd and Aunt Karyn were also there, eager to meet their new niece, the first granddaughter of both the Malchus and Flynn families. Phone calls were made. Pictures were taken. It was a joyous time.

Our only concern occurred early in the evening. At one point, you seemed to be having trouble breathing. Fortunately, a nurse was on hand to demonstrate how to help you cough up saliva you'd swallowed. It seemed simple — a slap on the back to dislodge it, and everything would be fine. When visiting hours ended, everyone left and we prepared to turn in, our hospital room becoming home for the night. As the hospital floor grew quiet and we were about to go to sleep, I looked down at you in your cradle. I realized that you were once again having trouble.

Lifting you to my shoulder, I followed the instructions given to me by the nurse. Try as I might, though, my efforts weren't successful, and you continued to gasp for air.

Like the hand of God reaching down, that same nurse happened to check on us before her shift ended. She smiled and took over for me, but after a couple attempts, her expression turned serious. She wrapped you in her arms and called out, "I'm taking this baby to the ICU."

And just like that, your mom and I were alone.

I stood in shock. Your mom, bedridden from the surgery, finally blurted, "Go. You have to go with her, Scott." Walking blindly to the nurses' station, I was directed around a corner to the secure doors of the Neonatal Intensive Care Unit. For the first time in my life, I didn't hear a song circling around in my head. No happy melodies to bring me solace. There was only silence. To enter the NICU, I had to speak through an intercom and have a nurse buzz me in. An eternity passed between pressing the intercom button and someone answering.

As I spoke, my voice was unfamiliar. I was in a dream. No, it was a nightmare. This couldn't be happening. You were just born! The doors swooshed open, and a nurse intercepted me, giving instructions to sterilize my hands in a long metal sink. She then took me into a small waiting area where a television was broadcasting some inane reality program. I caught a glimpse, however, of a doctor and nurses gathered around you, my tiny daughter, working furiously. I sat staring at the TV, not knowing what to do, not knowing how to act. One thing that never entered my mind was whether you'd live or die because you couldn't *die. I wouldn't let it happen.*

Finally, the doctor came over and greeted me, wearing a look of relief. "She gave us quite a scare," he said, a slight smile on his face. He must have been happy to save a life that night. While he explained in pseudo-layman's terms what had transpired, my only thought was "Take me to Sophie." He led me to you, laying in a Plexiglas case with monitors attached to your skin and an IV pumping antibiotics into your fragile arm.

When I finally returned to your mom's bedside, I fumbled my way through the doctor's explanation. Tests were being done to make sure you didn't have a heart defect (which you didn't) and that your lungs were healthy (which they were). Most importantly, you were okay. The two of us prayed, and then we tried to sleep. Eerily, at exactly midnight, the clock in our room stopped. After what we'd been through over the previous 24 hours, you'll have to forgive our superstition.

I raced back to the ICU to make sure all was well. You were fine. Back in the room, I called your Uncle Budd, and my voice must have been full of dread, because he shouted, "What happened?" That's when I broke down in tears.

Early in the morning I wheeled your mom into the NICU. Frightening as it had felt the night before, it turned out we were the lucky ones. All around us, smaller, frailer infants (most of them preemies) lay in their own cases, each with longer roads ahead of them. We stared at you, our precious baby, and squeezed hands. From the nurses' station, a small transistor radio played an innocuous soft rock song. It was surprisingly soothing. As the song faded out, the familiar piano intro to Bryan Adams' "(Everything I Do) I Do It for You" began. Julie and I looked at each other. How appropriate that this song of devotion and love would be playing at that moment. You see, at that point, I really began to feel the weight and responsibility — and the pain and the joy and the love — of being a parent. I thought to myself, "This child will look to me for guidance and inspiration — and, of course, love. I will do my best provide her with a good life, a fulfilling life."

You would spend another seven days in the hospital, and I can't describe how empty and sad it was to return to our apartment without you. It was a bittersweet homecoming. When you did arrive home, the three of us all snuggled on the couch. At long last, we could begin the life as a family we'd waited so long to start.

A couple of weeks later, I was browsing through a record store, an old habit that I often used to clear my head. I came across the CD single for that Bryan Adams song. I didn't think twice about purchasing it, no matter what kind of look the Gen-X store clerk gave me. I wasn't sure how often I would listen to "(Everything I Do) I Do It For You," but I knew it belonged in our record collection.

Everything I do, I'll do it for you and your brother, Sophie. Only, I'm not able to do it with the raspy voice of Bryan Adams, the thunder of a "Mutt" Lange snare drum, or heartfelt strings arranged by the late Michael Kamen. Oh, I know there are hipper, cooler songs out there that I could dedicate to you, Sophie. But aren't most songs that fathers dedicate to their daughters cheesy anyway? At least this one was co-written and produced by the guy who worked the boards for AC/DC and Def Leppard and another guy who arranged strings for David Gilmour and Metallica.

The truth of the matter is you don't choose a song like this one. When it's two in the morning, you're numb from the train that hit you early that night, and your wife, who cannot stand, is lying by your side while you gaze upon the miracle that is your child, whatever song that comes on the little radio in the NICU has the potential to become a part of you. For the rest of my life, I'll no longer associate Bryan Adams' masterpiece (if you can call it that) with the mediocre Robin Hood movie starring Kevin Costner, and I can forget the millions of times I heard it in the summer of '91.

Roll your eyes all you want, Sophie, but this work of melodic rock power balladry will always be your song.

THE BUGGLES
"VIDEO KILLED THE RADIO STAR"

Despite what some people may think, the Buggles were not an up-an-coming band when MTV aired the promotional film to their prophetic song, "Video Killed the Radio Star," as the first ever music video on the network. In fact, the song was already two years old and the members of the Buggles, Trevor Horn and Geoff Downes, had joined the prog rock band Yes and watched that group break up before the world ever saw "Video Killed the Radio Star." A minor hit in the U.S. in the late 1970s, I was fortunate to hear it on occasion thanks to great Cleveland radio stations like WMMS and WGCL.

I was always very fond of the song, not just for novelty's sake. The melody is tinged with melancholy and the beautiful piano coda is quite moving. "Video Killed the Radio Star" had enough of a lasting impression on me that I sought it out during my obsession with '80s New Wave that overcame me in the early 1990s. Within a three month period, I bought eight or nine of the *Rock of the 80's* cassettes released by Priority Records. These collections provided the background music to the first screenplay I wrote. Once the script was completed, the tapes went into a box and onto a shelf in a closet. By that time, my CD collection had grown big enough to make my cassettes obsolete.

When 21st century technology made it possible to convert those old cassettes into compact discs, I was eager to sift through my *Rock of the 80's* compilations and create a mix CD of my favorite tracks. One of the first songs I included was the Buggles "Video Killed the Radio Star." Unfortunately, the CD I burned was incompatible with my home stereo so the only place I could listen to it was in our car. This is how Sophie discovered her first rock song.

During Sophie's toddler years, as I was trying to wean her off of Barney (like any good parent should), I would slap in that '80s mix CD whenever we drove around town. Although I tried to 'get her interested in all of the songs, she never wanted to hear Pete Townshend or the Fixx. She wanted the Buggles and the "Ohwa-Oh's" from "Video Killed the Radio Star." Wherever we went, I knew I could comfort her with the Buggles, whether it was after a rough morning on the way to daycare, off to her cousin's house or just to the grocery store. Like many children, she misheard the lyrics to the chorus and would sing "video *wed* the radio star." I've always found her lyrical misinterpretation to be much more optimistic than the original song. It also made the song more personal. No longer was this just a nostalgic one-hit-wonder from my childhood; it belonged to Sophie's.

Finding a song like that was particularly resourceful during the long October of 2001, just before Jacob was born. Julie was hospitalized twice, the second time for two weeks on bed rest. The hospital was thirty minutes from home, daycare twenty-five minutes and my office at least an hour. Sophie and I spent a lot of time driving. Just a few months shy of turning three-years-old, she didn't understand why her mommy was in the hospital or why her daddy would walk around with heavy footfalls, constantly running his hand through his hair. These unknowns stressed her out, causing many tears, hugs and heavy hearts. Most of those nights I would snuggle her to sleep in the big bed of our empty house, praying that the next day would be easier.

Thankfully we had music to ease our pain. We had the Wiggles, *Dragon Tales*, *Sesame Street*, and we had the Buggles.

During that difficult period, it often felt like I was leaning on Sophie's tiny shoulders to keep me standing. I have never told her how important it was having her with me during that time. I'm not sure she'd understand. Sometimes I look at Sophie and I'm mystified that she's my child. I see a girl that is loving, caring, smart, quizzical, funny, and one who has an abundance of empathy. Simply put, she is amazing.

I often wonder, "Does she even remember that time? Does she even remember what we listened to?" A few months ago, I loaded

Julie's iPod with music and included "Video Killed the Radio Star" along with the other most-requested song from those trips in the car, Marshall Crenshaw's "Someday, Someway." One night, the Crenshaw number came on and I glanced at Sophie with a smile.

"What?" she asked.

I furrowed my brow. "Don't you remember?"

"No. What?"

When I explained to her the significance of the song, she bopped her head a little, semi-interested, then said, "Oh, okay."

Last week, "Video Killed the Radio Star" began playing. Once again, I looked her way. This time Sophie was smiling.

"You know this song?" I asked, uncertain.

"Yeah. I used to listen to it when I was younger."

THE BEATLES
"HERE COMES THE SUN"

The phone rang sometime in the middle of the day. I was at my desk prepping materials for an upcoming record session at the animation company where I worked. It was busywork to keep my mind occupied while I awaited this call from Julie. She had taken our son, Jacob, then under a month old, to see the pediatrician. Jacob's failure to thrive had been a cause for concern, and the doctor wanted to rule out the disease cystic fibrosis as the cause of his lack of growth. It was early December 2001.

When I answered, I could hear it in Julie's voice that she was fighting back tears. What we had feared was confirmed…

Jacob did indeed have cystic fibrosis.

Cystic fibrosis (CF) is an inherited chronic disease that affects approximately 30,000 children and adults in the United States (70,000 worldwide). Due to a defective gene and the protein it produces, a CF patient's body produces thick, sticky mucus that clogs the lungs and obstructs the pancreas. This mucus can lead to life-threatening lung infections that must be combated daily with a regimen of medicines inhaled via a nebulizer machine, as well as percussive vibrations on the chest and back, usually performed with a device called the Vest. Because the pancreas is obstructed, the natural enzymes used to help the body break down and absorb food are ineffective. A CF patient must take supplemental enzymes with each meal and snack.

The CF gene was discovered in the late '80s, leading to advancements in treating the disease. While medications have bettered and prolonged the lives of people who live with the disease, it is still a daily battle to stay both physically and emotionally healthy.

Julie and I were familiar with some of this CF information following the dramatic events of Jacob's birth. He was delivered at thirty-six weeks and immediately placed in the Neonatal Intensive Care Unit at the same Burbank hospital where Sophie was delivered and had her own stay in the NICU. After he was born, it was determined that Jacob's intestines were blocked by a meconium plug which was preventing him from having a bowel movement. The NICU doctor wanted to operate and remove the obstruction, but when no operating room was available the morning of the scheduled procedure, our tiny infant son was loaded onto a helicopter and flown to UCLA Medical Center where a *different* doctor would do the operation.

We packed up our things, and even though Julie was still recovering from a C-section, prepared to relocate. Sophie was placed in the care of her aunt and uncle while we drove across town to UCLA. Maybe it was the altitude from the helicopter ride, or perhaps it was some higher power stepping it to stop an unneeded medical procedure, but Jacob finally passed the meconium and the operation was put on hold. Two days later, we were discharged from the hospital. This incident seemed just a bump in the road, and we were on our way home to become the typical American family.

The morning Jacob was released from UCLA, the surgeon spoke to us, the first and only time we met him. It was a routine exchange of information, and although I tried to focus on everything he said, I really just wanted to go home. Then he made a comment that pricked my ears: he said that he believed a cystic fibrosis test had been administered and that he'd forward the results to our pediatrician. Those two words registered somewhere in the corner of my memory. Wasn't cystic fibrosis the disease my cousin Kenny's son had? Wasn't that the disease that took his son's life when he was just a boy?

I tabled those thoughts for the time being. Jacob was coming home, that's what mattered. "Everything is fine," we thought.

Obviously, it wasn't.

On that December afternoon, when I hung up the phone with Julie, my initial thought was, "I should have been there." Julie shouldn't have been alone to receive this news. But deep down we didn't believe it was CF. It had to be a virus or something easily treatable. The optimist in me was certain Jacob *would* be fine, because everything always seemed to work out for us.

Damn it, I was so wrong. I should have been there.

I told my boss the news, and as I spoke those words, "cystic fibrosis," I felt removed from my body, as if watching myself in a movie. This unreal feeling continued for the next hour as I left work and drove home. I could only imagine what Julie had experienced. She described the room beginning to spin and the doctor's words swirling around her head, try as she might to remain composed.

I should have been there.

Information I'd picked up from the Internet ran through my head. Clogged lungs? Malnutrition? One fact cut the deepest: Statistics had the average life expectancy of a CF patient living into his/her early 30's. Dear Christ, I was 32 years old. Was it possible that my precious boy would not make it to *his* 32nd birthday? How could that be?

When I arrived home, I walked in the front door and found Julie. I just wanted to hold her and the kids. I felt like if we curled up in a ball, this dream would end and we would awaken the next day to a different test result. You become a parent with an understanding that there will be challenges every single day, but the challenges will be worth it because of the love you get in return from your child. It was difficult to wrap my head around this bigger challenge. Yes, I would never waver from being there for my son, but what did the future hold? Was I a weaker father for even questioning these things? That's how I felt.

The rest of the evening was spent making phone calls. Our friends and family offered encouragement along with promises to be there whenever we needed them. My mom said she would drive out from Tucson at the drop of a hat while Julie's mother was ready to hop on a plane. When I called my friend Matt, he was speechless. Normally a man full of an unabridged dictionary of words, he suddenly had none. Of all the conversations I had that night, I won't forget the call I got from my cousin Kenny, telephoning from his home in Alabama. Even though Kenny's beloved son had lost the battle with CF, Kenny was the most hopeful person I spoke to that night. He told me of the advances made to prolong the lives of people with CF and better their quality of life. This man, who had suffered so much, was trying to lift Julie and me up.

It took some time for me to realize how gracious it was for Kenny to make that call. Julie and I soon learned that all CF families support each other, and the day Jacob was diagnosed we had instantly become members of a much larger family. Sadly, it's one we wish we *weren't* a part of.

2001 crawled to an end. Whatever holiday cheer we mustered was dampened by the news about Jacob. Thank God for Sophie and her cousins to remind us of the joy and love of the holiday season.

We didn't travel to Ohio that year and spent our first Christmas in the new house. I tried to hold on to my optimism, to counter our fears with a determination to make sure Jacob would outlive everyone. Throughout this period, I found myself humming George Harrison's "Here Comes the Sun" from the Beatles album, *Abbey Road*. Harrison was in the news as he'd succumbed to cancer in late November which is perhaps why I found myself with the song on my mind. Or perhaps it was because my brother, Budd, had latched on to the song, sometimes saying to me, "Hey, bro, here comes the son," when referring to Jacob. At other times, I know he was expressing the hopefulness of the composition.

During that sad, tearful Christmas season, one moment remains frozen in my memory. It was this night that "Here Comes the Sun" played on the stereo in our living room while Budd held Jacob up in the air, my son's tiny frame swimming in a onesie. Budd stared at him with such intensity, as if he might be able to will the illness out of Jacob's body, before handing Jacob off and leaving the room to collect himself, away from the rest of us. It was only one of a couple occasions that I've ever seen Budd tear up.

"Here Comes the Sun" quickly became one of Jacob's anthems. The same optimism that Harrison sang about is the same optimism that our family has that a cure for CF is just over the horizon. Since Jacob was diagnosed, our family of friends and relatives have been involved with many fundraisers, from our yearly participation in the national CF Foundation fundraiser, Great Strides, to running marathons, climbing stairs, selling hats and even holding a couple screenings of *King's Highway*, the feature movie that I wrote and directed. Our efforts may sound like a lot of work, but it never feels that way.

When your child has an illness, especially one that seems so close to a cure, you willingly do anything you can to make sure that he will see many, many more sunrises in his lifetime.

BRUCE SPRINGSTEEN
SOPHIE'S SPRINGSTEEN TAPE

Bruce Springsteen released his 12th studio album, *The Rising*, in July 2002, beginning a creative streak that has not let up in ten years. With the U.S. still reeling from the 9/11 terrorist attacks and stories of fallen soldiers in the headlines, the Boss recorded a masterful reflection on loss, sorrow, love, hope, redemption and trying to find one's way through the darkness. Each song stands up with his finest material from an extraordinary career that dates back to 1973. Making the album even more compelling was the fact that Springsteen recorded *The Rising* with the fabled E Street Band for the first time since the early 1980s sessions that resulted in *Born in the USA*. Springsteen fans rejoiced, as this was what we'd been waiting for since Springsteen and the E Street Band had reunited for a triumphant tour in 1999.

At that time in the life of my family, we were coming to grips with our own feelings of hopelessness, sorrow, anger, love, hope and struggles with faith. It was a mere seven months after Jacob had been diagnosed with cystic fibrosis. Personally, I had bottled up many of the fears and doubts that had taken up residency in my mind, foolishly assuming that Julie would not want to discuss *my* feelings because *she* was going through the same emotions. There were many times I wound up crying alone, either secluded in my car, on the couch, or quietly at night while my wife slept next to me.

Just as I'd done throughout my life, I turned to music to help me through some of those dark times. More than any album I listened to, *The Rising* tapped into the well of feelings I was experiencing. In many ways, it saved me. What *The Rising* also did was bring the music of Bruce Springsteen into the hearts of my children and create a special bond for our family, providing joy and inspiration for all four of us.

The album was a critical and commercial success. In true Springsteen fashion, he and the E Street Band toured the world, including a stop in Barcelona, Spain that was filmed and broadcast on European television. Around the time of the 2003 Grammy Awards, for which *The Rising* received multiple nominations, the CBS TV network aired an hour of the Barcelona concert footage to drum up anticipation for the awards show.

I freakishly set up the VCR to record the program on the Friday night it aired. Sophie watched in fascination as her wild-eyed fanatical father pressed buttons and frantically searched for a blank VHS tape. She asked what I was doing, and I explained that I was taping the Springsteen concert. Excited, Sophie told me she wanted to watch "The Springsteen."

It was a little dishearteningly when, the next morning, the first thing she asked to watch was...*Rugrats*. But it was okay, because the *next* thing she wanted to see was, yes, "The Springsteen."

Feeding off of my enthusiasm, Jacob agreed to forego his favorite music videos during his morning breathers therapy. At the time, he only liked the Wiggles (or "Wiwis," as he called them) and Sesame Street. Together the three of us watched The Springsteen, and my kids loved it. Once his breathers were completed, Jacob insisted on replaying the performance of "Dancing in the Dark." Free of his Vest and nebulizer tubes, he danced around the room, mimicking Springsteen's manic behavior. As for Sophie, she fell in love with violinist Soozie Tyrell. In a matter of days, my little girl created her own "violin" by taking a recorder, pulling off the bottom piece and shoving a drumstick in the end. Tucking it under her chin, she'd hold her violin with her left hand and use a second drumstick as the bow. I was on cloud nine having introduced my children, a new generation, to the music of an artist who had inspired me since my senior year of high school.

A month or so later, Sophie requested her own Springsteen mix tape. I leapt at the opportunity and created "Sophie's Springsteen Tape," incorporating the upbeat songs from the CBS special (there would be time for the sad songs later in life) along with an assortment of Bruce classics every child should know: "Badlands," "Give the

Girl a Kiss," "Seaside Bar Song," and "Glory Days," just to name a few. Through long road trips and short drives around town, Sophie and Jacob sang along to the choruses from "Lonesome Day" and "The Rising." They would bounce their heads to "Lion's Den" and scream "the change was made uptown and the Big Man joined the band" from "Tenth Avenue Freeze Out." My children knew who Clarence Clemons was. The Big Man! How cool is that? Eventually they came to know all of the E Street Band: Max, Garry, Nils, Patti, Danny, the Professor and Little Stevie.

Their favorite song may have been "Mary's Place." During this rousing number, Sophie misheard the chorus, singing "Meet me at the wedding place," which I always felt gave the song a touch of innocence. During the last verse, as the music quiets and the back-up singers begin calling out "Turn it up," Julie made it a tradition to literally turn up the music with each call out, then quickly back down again. This made the kids ecstatic each and every time, and they would laugh and sing with all of their hearts. I can't tell you how many times we listened to that tape in our van over a two-year period, until it finally got tangled and snapped from having being loved to death.

In a year that found my children beginning a journey into Springsteen fandom, 2003 also took our family on a journey from our California home to the beaches of Hawaii. Julie and I were already involved with the CF Foundation's yearly fundraiser, Great Strides, but I wanted to do more. People knew so little about cystic fibrosis, and I felt the urge to educate and raise more money for the cause. At a CF parents function in March I was handed a pamphlet about marathon training. In a moment of clarity, a single word came to me:

Run.

I could run a marathon and raise money for the CF Foundation! By writing letters about my goal I could educate friends and family, and by punishing my body, I could inspire people to donate and help the efforts to find a cure for CF. It was a crazy thought, especially given the fact that I hadn't been a dedicated runner since my high school cross-country days, although "dedicated" is a big stretch when describing my teenage athleticism. Nevertheless, sixteen years after the last time I'd run more than two miles, the idea of running twenty-six-point-two of them was an epiphany. In fact, it felt like a calling. And so, I signed up to run the Honolulu Marathon.

Julie, Sophie, Jacob and I flew to Hawaii in December, 2003. As any amateur marathon runner will tell you, that first marathon is an exhilarating experience. It doesn't matter how fast you run or where you finish, it's the sense of accomplishment you receive once you cross the finish line. Think about it: after months of training and raising $10,000 for the CF Foundation, I was going to be running twenty-six (point two) freaking miles! The exotic sights of the island only heightened the experience, from the sun rising over the mountains to the vast ocean and the tropical foliage.

The highlight of my race wasn't the sight-seeing, though. It came at the dreaded twenty-second mile, "the wall," as runners call it. I was met at that point in the race by my trainer, Robert, who jogged alongside me for that offensive mile, the whole time offering words of encouragement and distracting me from the cramp in my side and the aches in my feet. During our short time on the road together, Robert called Julie on her cell phone.

"We love you," she said, her voice full of excitement. Speaking to the love of my life gave me the extra boost I needed when I thought I might keel over. Pushing forward, I sang to myself the Springsteen songs that I'd taught my children, the very melodies that filled my heart with love, that buoyed me across the finish line to collapse into the arms of my family.

After the race, we began a weeklong stay in Hawaii. It was one of the greatest vacations ever. Unlike our trips to Cleveland or Tucson to visit family, this time it was just the four of us. In that tranquil tropical environment, our lives were on hold, as if the troubles and fears that were a part of our daily routine had been left back in California while we basked in the sun and splashed in the turquoise ocean.

At week's end, Julie and I wanted mementos for the kids to remind them of our tropical holiday. Sophie and Jacob asked for ukuleles. The size of the instrument was perfect for their little hands, and thus they became the kids' "guitars."

Once we returned home, the children continued watching The Springsteen on a regular basis, Sophie with her homemade violin and Jacob with his ukulele/guitar. They would prance around the living room, singing along to their favorite songs. Sometimes I would imagine them learning to play the actual instruments and jamming with the *real* E Street Band. Hey, a father can dream, can't he?

"Sophie's Springsteen Tape," and its replacement, "Sophie and Jake's Springsteen CD," kind of ruined my listening experience of *The Rising*. Whenever I hear the title track, I expect to hear "Mary's Place," followed by "Lonesome Day," instead of the original track listing. I don't mind, though (sorry, Bruce), because that mix tape not only made the music of Springsteen an important part of Sophie and Jacob's childhood but provided many lasting memories. On days when I'm melancholy and I feel that elephant sitting on my chest, I think back to that Hawaiian trip and recall the light in the eyes of my children, or I conjure the sound of their voices singing Springsteen. Although many years have passed since that time, all it takes to place me in the right frame of mind is to imagine Sophie singing, "Meet me at the wedding place!"

That's the power of music, my friends.

That's the power of Bruce Springsteen.

PATTY GRIFFIN
"HEAVENLY DAY"

Slow dancing. It's something Julie and I did more frequently in the early years of our marriage. There we'd be, alone in our apartment, holding each other and swaying to the music of Bonnie or Shawn or Bruce or Ella. Outside, you could hear the helicopters buzzing over North Hollywood or rowdy neighbors socializing in the courtyard below. But as the music played on, the real world would fade away, and it was just the two of us in our own paradise. The arrival of children and professional careers made our lives busier and those simple times more infrequent. These days our nights are spent filling in the details of our workdays and getting the kids ready for bed. If we're lucky, there's time to sink into the couch and spend a half hour or so involved with some mindless sitcom. The days of dancing seemed far-gone, until we heard Patty Griffin's beautiful "Heavenly Day."

You may not know who Patty Griffin is, but you've probably heard her music sung by the likes of the Dixie Chicks ("Let Him

Fly"), Miranda Lambert ("Getting Ready") or Kelly Clarkson ("Up to the Mountain (MLK Song)." Julie and I became fans the moment we heard her 1996 debut album, *Living with Ghosts.* With just her guitar and voice, that record ranks as one of the best first records in the past twenty years. Griffin's songs, "Every Little Bit," "You Are Not Alone," and the tragic "Poor Man's House" received some airplay on the L.A. radio station we listened to back in the mid-1990s. After the station was sold and changed formats, Griffin's subsequent albums were ditched in the corporate downsizing of A&M Records (who dropped her after Universal bought the label), finding her music became a challenge.

Fortunately, there were champions of Patty Griffin, from Emmylou Harris and the Dixie Chicks to bloggers like Jeff Giles and half the staff of Popdose.com. The singer eventually found a new home at ATO Records, which has allowed her a chance to continue growing and succeeding as an artist. What I adore about Patty Griffin is the conviction with which she sings every song. Few artists can match her intensity and soul both on record and in concert (where she excels). After signing to ATO, Griffin went to work and released a three stunning albums: *1,000 Kisses* (2002), *Impossible Dreams* (2004), and *Children Running Through* (2007), the CD where you'll find "Heavenly Day."

The execs at ATO were savvy enough to realize that the old models of getting a musician's work into the public's ear have fallen by the wayside. Because radio seems to have an aversion to folk-based music, they approached music supervisors for films and television series with their artists' repertoire. It was while watching a quirky romantic series called *Side Order of Life* that Julie and I first heard "Heavenly Day." Among other topics, this Lifetime series dealt with one character's battle against cancer. During the final moments of a particularly emotional episode, the character decided to take charge of her life in the face of the deadly disease and cut off her curly locks just before starting chemotherapy. However, when it came time to cut her hair, she couldn't lift the scissors. Her best friend, standing by, lifted the shears for her and proceeded to start the cutting. Against these images, "Heavenly Day" played. While it was devastating to watch, Griffin's lyrics provided an uplifting message, perhaps revealing the ill woman's optimism and fighting spirit.

Expecting television viewers to focus on the screen action while a song like this one plays is a risk. Griffin steals your attention with a voice so compelling and music so wondrous. But it's not like your mind is being diverted. Unlike so many of Griffin's potent compositions, "Heavenly Day" pierces the heart with joy instead of melancholy. For obvious reasons, Julie and I have found comfort in the song's message. Any family dealing with the daily stress and worry of having a loved one living with an illness can embrace "Heavenly Day" and celebrate its positive message.

In truth, this song really belongs to Julie; she's listened to it hundreds more times than I have. It does not affect me the way it does her. But isn't that how many songs become our own, too? We find music that becomes vital to us not only through a single moment or years of moments, but also through the people with whom we associate the songs.

Looking back on those early years of marriage when Julie and I would create our own private ballroom, I have no clue what exact track was playing accompaniment to our slow dances. However, I *can* tell you what song was playing the most recent time we held each other and danced. We'd just returned home from an evening excursion to get ice cream after a long, tiring day. While Sophie and Jacob sat in the kitchen gobbling up their frozen goodies, Julie turned on the stereo and pulled me close. There we were, alone in our living room, swaying to the music of Patty Griffin. As one of our favorite artists sang, Sophie and Jacob carried on their own conversation.

"I like vanilla."

"Yeah, it's good."

"Oooh, brain freeze."

And then giggling.

It was perfect. It was a heavenly day.

U2

"RUNNING TO STAND STILL"

Like a long-lost brother, Elliott greeted me with a warm hug as I stepped into his house. Although it had only been six months since we last saw one another, the passage of time felt like years. He looked the same: stocky, glasses, curly hair and a funky goatee sprouting from his chin. His eyes had the creases of sadness that began the morning he learned that his older brother, Matt, had died; creases which would sink deeper when his father passed away nearly a year later. Elliott and I shared an uncommon bond: We had both lost Matt, who was my oldest friend and a brother to me. Elliott and I had begun talking regularly after Matt died in 2005, but only recently had we become friends in our own right. No longer did all of our conversations involve the topics of death or of those we knew who were dying. Instead, we shot the shit about stupid subjects like Journey, great movies we'd seen and new music we liked.

We grinned and made some ice-breaking smartass remarks before entering the kitchen to sit at the same table I had known from my childhood. The smell of ancient cigarettes hung in the air from decades of Camels and Marlboros inhaled by Elliott, Matt and their father. Even though Elliott now sequestered himself to the garage to light up, that sweet tobacco aroma would never go away. Elliott grabbed a couple of Bud Lights and slid one to me across the table. As we cracked open the beers, I took comfort in the familiarity of this house I called my second home during my childhood and adolescence.

Elliott's mom, Mrs. B, was off getting made up, as if my visit was of some importance. Who was I other than that punk who had always hung out with her son? At least, that's how I felt. While Elliott and I waited for her, the two of us got caught up, filling in the gaps of our lives that didn't come up during our once-a-month rambling phone calls. Mrs. B finally popped her head in to say "hello" and give a hug. Still dressed in her bathrobe, she looked as if life was treating her well. The past few years had been devastating, yet she seemed to be surviving. Then she rushed off to finish getting ready while Elliott heated the oven for a steak lunch he was cooking for us.

As the meat broiled, Elliott sheepishly brought out his acoustic guitar and strummed a few chords. My mind flashed to one of my favorite photos of Matt taken just before he moved to Seattle in 1993. In it, he's holding a guitar, his long wavy hair dangling in his face. Through thick, round glasses his eyes are full of life, and he's giving the camera a wide grin. The edges of the picture are fuzzy, possibly because it was the last photo on the roll.

And now here was Elliott, holding his own guitar the same way, strands of hair hanging in his face the same way, and his eyes casting that same full-of-life look.

"Play him that song you wrote!" Mrs. B called out from her bedroom at the back of the house, her voice full of pride.

Elliott rolled his eyes and shouted back, "Right, mom," then ignored her request.

Instead, the chords he played had a familiar ring to them and when he began singing a hushed version of U2's "Running to Stand Still," I had to look away for fear I might cry. U2 was one of those bands I associated with Matt, and since his death, I rarely listened to their music. This particular song, with its torn innocence and building passion, always reminded me of him, even while he was alive. When *The Joshua Tree* was released in 1987, "Running to Stand Still" was often played during the times Matt and I would hang out in my basement or while driving around town in the Whomobile. We had seen it performed live in the autumn of '87 at the old Cleveland Municipal Stadium during U2's world tour. Elliott was with us for that concert, and so the song connects all three of us.

He finished the U2 number, and we looked at each other. After a long silence, I requested he play his original song, which he got halfway through before the oven timer went off. He never finished playing the song for me, but it was quite good.

Mrs. B rejoined us, now officially dressed for my visit. She opened a bottle of wine and expressed her excitement about the future, including her impending retirement. I was surprised that she did not seem overly annoyed with the twelve-foot wall the city had constructed in her backyard to reduce traffic noise. Building it had required the plowing down of the forest where Matt and I had once stashed skin magazines we'd stolen from under his dad's bed. As the wine flowed and the lunch was devoured, we talked and laughed and reminisced. It was comical watching Elliott and Mrs. B interact as they have developed a unique relationship, something out of a David Lynch film. They bicker, finish each other's sentences, tease one another and correct each other's mistakes, but under all of their words and actions permeates a deep love, a bond only they can understand.

Mrs. B got up to answer the phone while Elliott and I wandered back to his room to check out a documentary about cinematographers that he'd recorded. We went about things as if this was just another day, two friends hanging out, drinking, watching some TV and listening to good tunes. He played me a recording of Bob Dylan reciting a poem about the death of Woody Guthrie. The free flowing words from a young Dylan swirled around in my brain as I tried to grasp their meaning. These same words, lost on me, resonated with Elliott and brought him to tears.

While I toiled away at sampling the music of artists on Elliott's iPod, he went out for a smoke and to refresh our drinks. He returned with a sad smile and said, "My mom's out there crying. It means so much when you come to visit."

Who was I? I wasn't just that punk who had always hung out with her son. I was his best friend, his brother. She feels connected to Matt through me, and I am a reminder that other people loved Matt and that he had affected lives. I stammered, trying to find the proper response, but Elliott cut me off, saying, "We both do."

As my visit was winding down, Mrs. B came into Elliott's room to give me a hug. She placed a twenty-dollar bill in my hand, insisting I take it and put it to good use. I looked at Elliott, who shrugged. After she exited, he told me, "She'll be insulted if you don't keep it." Always the mother.

Elliott saw me to the front door. He embraced me once more and slapped me on the back, a last hug until the next time we saw each other. Walking to my car, daylight was quickly fading under a pasty-gray sky.

I backed the car into the street, waved one last time to Elliott before he closed the front door, then I drove off into the evening singing U2.

EDDIE VEDDER
"HARD SUN"

As the latest round of California wildfires burned on in cities near our home, we waited anxiously to see whether the 2009 Pasadena Marathon would be canceled. For seven months, I'd trained for the half-marathon, enduring physical pain, spiritual drain and the stress of trying to raise more money for the Cystic Fibrosis Foundation. Halfway through the day, we learned that all direct routes to Pasadena from our house were closed, blocked by the fires and the crews battling them. With the air quality in question, there was a good chance that the race would be postponed or even scrapped altogether. We probably wouldn't be driving to Pasadena and spending the night in that lovely city, which left Sophie and Jacob very disappointed. They had looked forward to a weekend getaway, even if it was just 20 miles south of our home.

Yet, even if the half marathon was canceled, a sense of obligation told me that I would be running the next day, whether it was in Pasadena or in our hometown of Santa Clarita. It wasn't because I didn't want all of the training to be for naught; no, it was that I'd made a commitment to run for the CF Foundation and for all victims of the disease. I'd made a commitment to run for my son. Furthermore, the day the race fell on, November 16th, was chosen because of its proximity to Jacob's birthday. I felt it was a sign to be running for CF so close to his special day. Not only that but I couldn't suffer a postponement and go on training. My soul was tired, and my shoes had literally broken down. They were on their last legs. The show *had* to go on.

So I decided to map out my own 13.1-mile course, just in case there was no Pasadena Half Marathon the next morning.

Jacob tagged along as I drove around the city, noting landmarks for each mile until a half-marathon course was created. Eventually Jake dozed off, and I listened to some of the inspirational songs I had programmed into my iPod to help get me through the run, starting off with Eddie Vedder's "Hard Sun." If you're unfamiliar with this number, it was originally written by a Canadian singer-songwriter, Gordon Peterson, under the moniker, Indio. Vedder recorded a cover of it for Sean Penn's moving adaptation of the Jon Krakauer book, *Into the Wild*. The book and the movie follow the real-life adventures of Christopher McCandless, a college graduate who gave up all of his possessions and moved to Alaska to live off the land. Vedder's version of the song perfectly evokes the longing and searching of McCandless, as portrayed by Emile Hirsch in the film. The folksy approach he took to the score of the movie is no less potent than any of the hard rock songs Vedder writes with his band, Pearl Jam. His passion is what makes him one of the most dynamic singers of my generation and one of the most important songwriters of the past two decades.

Yet, like any great song, the meaning of "Hard Sun" transcends its connection with the source material. Its message feels more universal even though Vedder's inspiration was the book and the film.

I can only think of Julie when Vedder humbly speaks of the woman who makes him a better man. Through all of our years of marriage, she has brought out the best in me. When I'm with her, I want to be a better man. As much as I had been training to find a cure for Jacob, I would also be running for Julie, to ease her pain. As much as I suffer from fear and worry, I know that she suffers more. If I could do just one thing for her, I would cure our son. But I'm no doctor. I'm no scientist.

The best I can do is run.

Saturday night, we went to bed without any news about the marathon. A mass e-mail would be sent out to all participants Sunday morning at 4 a.m. to notify them if the race was still on. If it was still a go, we'd load up the family and drive to Pasadena (the roads had since opened). If not, I'd probably get a couple hours of extra sleep before running my own private race. At 4:15 Sunday morning, I stumbled down the hall, tripped over one of our damn cats and flipped on the office light. My eyes half-open, the computer screen slowly came into focus as I logged on to the Internet. Waiting for me was that mass e-mail: the marathon was canceled. With a slight nod, I wandered back to bed.

By 8 o'clock I was up again, going through the preparations to run *my* half-marathon. There was little doubt in my mind that no matter how poor the air quality, no matter how hot the temperature, no matter how blustery the winds, I would be out there running, earning every dollar that had been donated for the event.

Julie and the kids made their way out to the living room as I donned my worn-out running shoes, adjusted my grungy shorts and pulled on my Jacob's Joggers hat. At 8:30 we all drove to the parking lot of the local Hollywood Video, my starting line. On the way over, I visualized the course Jake and I had laid out the previous day, began to recall specific precious moments to help me through the difficult moments of the run, and I imagined completing my race and collapsing into my family's arms.

Up above, a big hard sun beat down and I found myself feeling anxious, as if surrounded by thousands of runners at the starting line of an actual marathon. Even though there wouldn't be a starter's pistol or a medal waiting for me at the end, there would be a better reward: the excitement in my kids' eyes and the smile on my wife's face.

I was ready. I gave Sophie a hug, squeezed Jacob tightly and I kissed Julie goodbye.

With my headphones in place, I began listening to Eddie Vedder singing and took off running.

"For Good"
from the musical *Wicked*

Our house was overrun by witches. You'd think that in the 21st Century there would be some way to control witch infestation, but there was no stopping these mystical creatures from getting into our home.

In the winter of 2007, Julie and Sophie went to see the phenomenon known as *Wicked.* Seeing the Los Angeles production of the Tony Award-winning musical was so magical that the experience was relived day after day for nearly a year. The original cast recording, featuring Idina Menzel as Elphaba, the green-skinned, misunderstood future Wicked Witch of the West, and Kristin Chenoweth as Galinda, soon to be Glinda the Good Witch, was on a constant loop in our house. For the first time, I saw in Julie the kind of obsession some people display for artists like—oh, I don't know— Springsteen. Meanwhile, Sophie could be heard singing the music nearly every day for a year until she'd memorized every line and was able to recreate scenes from memory.

The snippets of music I paid attention to were very melodic, and I enjoyed them. But, honestly, I didn't understand what the big deal was. I didn't read the CD booklet or do any research on *Wicked,* so I only knew the basics: It's a rite-of-passage tale of how two young women, complete opposites, form a loving friendship and eventually become the famous characters from L. Frank Baum's classic book, *The Wonderful Wizard of Oz.* The play, based on Gregory Maguire's novel, *Wicked: The Life and Times of the Wicked Witch of the West,* had become a sensation of *Titanic* proportions.

As 2008 drew to a close, Julie and Sophie desperately wanted to see *Wicked* again since the L.A. production was set to close in mid-January '09. Adding to their enthusiasm was news that actresses Eden Espinosa and Megan Hilty, whom they'd seen as the leads in the '07 performance, would be returning to reprise their roles of Elphaba and Glinda, respectively. Julie and Sophie both insisted that Jacob and I had to see the play in order to fully comprehend its greatness. In lieu of a birthday party, Sophie asked if we could go see *Wicked,* and in mid-December, just before Christmas, our family drove into downtown Los Angeles to the historic Pantages Theater for a night on Broadway.

We took our seats: Julie and I next to each other, Jacob sitting to my right, Sophie to Julie's left. As the lights dimmed and the orchestra began, Jacob gripped my hand.

We were instantly transported to the Land of Oz, thanks to Winnie Holzman's sensitive script and the winning songs from Stephen Schwartz. I periodically glanced at Jacob, curious if he was getting scared. Instead, I saw my little boy sitting wide-eyed and awestruck at the wondrous things happening on stage while glorious melodies were performed. When the curtain lowered following the spectacular Act I ending song, "Defying Gravity" (in which actress Espinosa was hoisted into the air – flying – while beams of light burst out behind her), I was indeed happy and thrilled that we had come to the play.

Throughout my entire childhood, my parents took us to musicals. Not just the big shows that came through the Cleveland downtown theaters, but many local productions that were just as good as (and sometimes superior to) the Broadway touring productions. Sitting in the Pantages, watching *Wicked*, I was reminded how much I love live theater, how much I do love musicals, and how much I miss the opportunity to see them. I was so glad that Sophie and Jake were at least being exposed to something as beautiful and moving as *Wicked* and that I was able to sit there with my son and observe how much he was enjoying it. Someday he may recall that night with fondness, and it warms my heart that I was a part of it.

For Act II, we changed seats so that I could be next to Sophie. Because she was the *Wicked* veteran, I figured I would be able to just focus on the stage, not having to worry about whether the flying monkeys were too intense for her.

As the second act unfolded, I was continually surprised by the many twists and the clever ways the play tied into the whole mythology of Baum's original book, as well as the landmark MGM film from 1939. Moreover, it impressed me with its themes of tolerance, empowerment, acceptance, and most importantly, forgiveness. During several of the high drama moments, I couldn't resist seeing how Sophie was reacting. Looking at her, I was often more touched at her connection to the play than what was actually happening on stage. With her eyes locked in on the action, as if memorizing every gesture of the actresses, Sophie quietly sang along with each song, never looking away, never letting go of my hand.

The final scene between Glinda and Elphaba is a moving duet entitled "For Good." During the number, these two women, once hated roommates but now best friends, must say goodbye. In the song, the two admit that their lives are better for knowing each other and that they will never be the same. Out of context from the musical, "For Good" is a beautiful ballad that has universal appeal. I can already hear Sophie someday singing this at her high school graduation and hitting each note sincerely, a heartfelt dedication to her own friends. As Espinosa and Hilty crescendoed into the final chorus, it was the father squeezing his child's hand tighter and the *child* looking over to see her *father* fighting back tears, overwhelmed with joy.

In that moment, I understood.

I understood not only why this play has been so successful and connects with so many people emotionally, but why Julie and Sophie had effused over it for a year. Beyond that, I finally understood what it was like for all of the people I've dragged to their first Springsteen concerts and why they've always remarked after the show, "I get it."

I thanked God that I was able to be there, in that moment, experiencing the same emotions as my daughter.

After the show had ended and the house lights came on, as we joined the massive crowd making its way back to their cars in the chilly December air, the poignant melody of "For Good" sang on in my mind and my heart ached. Our time in Oz had been short and, well, quite wonderful. I was going to miss those characters and what we'd been through together. A play, very much like a concert, is a unique experience between the performers and the audience. No two nights are the same, no matter how well-rehearsed the production. I may see *Wicked* again someday (I know I'll see the film when it eventually gets made), but it will not be the same.

Still, whenever I hear Sophie's voice singing through the house, I'll always be reminded of the gift she gave me.

Going to see *Wicked* may have been a birthday present to her, but Sophie gave me a memory that I will cherish forever, a memory that has changed me for good.

SHAWN COLVIN AND MARY CHAPIN CARPENTER
"ONE COOL REMOVE"

Julie said she was waiting for me.

In 1994, outside of Alterian Studios, the special effects company where I worked, a cat delivered a litter underneath a pile of lumber, directly next to the area where we used fiberglass chemicals. To save these babies from cancerous fumes, they were moved to a safer location, but the mother never returned. A group of us divided up the kittens and when the runt, a squeaky ball of white fur with black and gray patches on her back and legs, was the only one unclaimed, Julie and I adopted her. We named her Doodle.

At first Doodle was so small that Julie could put her in the front pocket of her overalls. Over the next week or so, the kitten slept on the bed with us, or on my chest where she would knead me with her claws. When Doodle was hungry, she would "mew," which was pathetic and sweet at the same time. This all took place in our first apartment, the one-bedroom sweatbox located in North Hollywood.

Our other two cats, Otis and Ella, treated Doodle with indifference. Otis and Ella were skittish and wouldn't let us near them, thus Doodle became the type of pet we had always imagined owning. She was friendly, purred when you scratched her ears or butt and tolerated being picked up and danced around the living room. On hot afternoons when I tried to stay cool without moving, I'd often doze off with Doodle lying on my stomach. It was relaxing.

One day, I returned from work and she was missing. Then I heard her cries, as if she was trapped somewhere in the apartment. After a frantic search, I discovered that Doodle had wedged herself under our convertible couch and crawled into a crevice between the metal springs of the pull-out bed. If you've ever owned a convertible, you know how damn heavy they are and can imagine how much fun it was lifting the couch to get her out. It hadn't been a learning experience for Doodle, though, and she did this regularly until she got eventually got too big to squeeze under the couch.

As newlyweds, Julie and I had little money. We went out maybe once or twice a month and were quite content spending our Saturday nights at home, relaxing on the couch with Doodle close by, listening to Shawn Colvin singing Tom Waits' "Heart of a Saturday Night" or covering Greg Brown's "One Cool Remove," as a wonderful duet with Mary Chapin Carpenter. Colvin is one of those artists who is not only a fine songwriter, but also interprets other people's work with a degree of grace and beauty that makes the songs her own. I find her *Cover Girl* album, and the numerous contributions she's made to tribute albums, just as moving as any of her deeply felt personal songs.

When Sophie was born in 1999, Doodle became the cat that showed indifference. By then, she was the queen, lounging around most of the time. She was friendly enough to Sophie, although we had to make sure she stayed out of Sophie's crib; I believe Doodle thought it was some special bed we'd constructed for her.

Two years later we made the big move from apartment to house, which meant a new hallway to run up and down, rooms to hide in and an outdoor patio where the cats could bask in the sun as long as they wanted. Doodle tended to stay indoors, choosing the comfy pillows of the couch or our bed from which to continue her household queenship. Her reign, would soon end.

Late 2001 was very tense and full of a great deal of uncertainty, all centered around Jacob's birth and his diagnosis of CF. When one of the cats began urinating throughout the house, primarily in the living room, our stress level went through the roof. Not only did it smell horrendous, but it was unsanitary for a 3-year old and infant to be rolling around on piss-stained carpet. The problem was we didn't know which cat was behind the foul deeds. Doodle answered that question one night as I sat watching *Sportscenter*. With my feet propped on the coffee table, she trotted out to the living room, directly to the spot where all the peeing had been done. Then, with a look that said, "Hey, look at me, I can do whatever I want," she cleared her bladder. It was all I could do not to wring her neck. From then on, Doodle became an outdoor cat.

After that night, for seven years Doodle owned the patio. She often roamed through neighbors' yards (I'm not sure exactly where to), but each evening she returned to either reside, diva-like, on one of the metal patio chairs, squeeze herself between the air conditioning unit and the house (she always liked cramped spaces) or just lay in the dirt under the large tree in our backyard. When the sun went down and the air grew cooler, I'd bring her inside and place her in a kennel, to protect her from inclement weather and stray coyotes that sometimes wandered down from the hills. But Doodle preferred to remain outdoors, often sprinting back to the door the moment she was set down in the house. Outside, she could rule, and rule she did.

If another cat from the neighborhood dared enter our yard, Doodle became very territorial, growling and hissing to chase them off. Meanwhile, whenever a raccoon or possum would sneak up to eat her food, Doodle looked on with disinterest. It was as if she thought these wild creatures were beneath her and not worth the hassle. After all, she was *domesticated.* Either that or she was smart enough not to tussle with a huge 'coon.

Doodle remained a loyal and friendly cat, always rubbing against your leg and shedding her fur on your clothes. But last week, quite suddenly, Doodle began walking more slowly and looking feeble. We quickly realized that she had stopped eating and drinking her water. I've heard that cats know when their time on earth is up, and we could tell just by looking at her that she was dying. Doing all that we could to make her comfortable, the one thing that seemed to put her most at ease was holding her and petting her. By Saturday evening, her once strong "meow" was a weak "croak." When I laid her down to sleep that night, the assumption was that she'd pass away sometime in the wee hours of the morning. The next day, though, I was the last one out of bed and surprised to find Doodle still conscious, with Julie sitting beside her.

"She feels so cold," Julie remarked.

Doodle let out a few more of her warbled croaks, and I took her up in my arms. Looking into her eyes I knew she was close to the end. For the next half hour, I laid on the floor with Doodle on my chest, much in the same way I used to when she was a kitten. I stroked her head and back as her breath became more labored. A minute would pass in which she would be still, and then the old girl would gasp for air. This went on for ten minutes.

Silence, then a gasp, then silence, then a gasp.

Then just silence.

It's a strange feeling to hold a creature as life leaves its body. I hope in the afterlife that Doodle is lounging around in the glow of the eternal sun and I hope that she is at peace.

As I placed Doodle down and covered her with a blanket, Julie came over to me, and we looked at each other.

"She was waiting for you," she said.

BOB DYLAN
"'CROSS THE GREEN MOUNTAIN"

I dread an empty house. When Julie and the kids are out of town, as they were the week before Christmas, our home is too quiet. No matter how many televisions I have blaring or how loud my music is playing, those sounds can't replace the laughter of Sophie and Jacob or the rise and fall of my wife's voice when she's on the telephone. Used to be I looked forward to spending some time alone when they went away to visit relatives back east. As each year passes, though, the length of time I enjoy alone dwindles; I'm down to about 24 hours before I'm feeling lonely.

The Sunday before I was scheduled to fly out and meet my family in Ohio, I vacuumed, tinkered on the computer, watched some movie I can't recall and let my iPod shuffle throughout the night. That's when Bob Dylan's epic "'Cross the Green Mountain" was introduced to me, its haunting melody wrapping itself around me, comforting my winter blues. The song, originally recorded for the 2003 Civil War film, *Gods and Generals*, is one of Dylan's finest later works. Its existence went relatively unnoticed until he released it on his latest outtakes *Bootleg Series* compilation, *Tell Tale Signs*. For years, the master songwriter has been mocked for his nasally vocals and what sounds like a lack of interest in some of his deliveries. That's not the case with "'Cross the Green Mountain." Each note he reaches for, each word he sings is done with conviction and a sincerity that leaves a lasting impression long after the song's eight minute running time. And while he does this, his stellar band marches the song along with quiet elegance. The organ, the violin, the bow across the bass, and the strumming guitars make this song heavenly.

Dylan's Civil War tale could be about any war, as his aching voice and the worn down nature of his singing easily capture the essence of a soldier pining for home while he reflects on what may be his last battle, his last moments in life. The grace and beauty of "'Cross the Green Mountain" made me think of Julie, Sophie and Jacob, longing to be by their side.

On Christmas Eve, I flew into Cleveland, arriving in the mid-afternoon. Entering a house full of warm spirits and the aroma of home-cooked food, I received big hugs and kisses and quickly felt at peace. While I navigated around running, screaming children and narrow doorways, I couldn't take my eyes off of Julie. With each conversation I had and every cookie I nibbled, I found myself glancing around, past the backs of people's heads, just to watch the way she smiles and how her incredibly curly hair bounces when she laughs. I stood mesmerized as she walked across the room or pitched in to help her mom with the cooking. The rest of my vacation, I kept stealing these moments, constantly saying to myself, "I am so damn lucky."

The morning of New Year's Eve, we drove to Pennsylvania for my cousin's wedding, into a rural part of the state founded soon after the Revolutionary War. As we passed aged farms, cold cows and skeletal trees that had long lost their leaves, I hummed "'Cross the Green Mountain" and thought of the many homes I've had: North Olmsted, Bowling Green, North Hollywood, and Santa Clarita, CA. I turned to my wife riding beside me, and then I looked back at my children in the backseat.

I dread an empty house, because without Julie and Sophie and Jacob the house is just a building.

They make it complete.

They make it a home.

JOURNEY
"ONLY THE YOUNG"

In the fall of 1984, the Make-A-Wish Foundation contacted the band Journey. A 16-year old fan from Cleveland named Kenny Sykaluk was in the final days of his lifelong battle with cystic fibrosis. One of his dreams was to meet his musical idols. The members of Journey flew to Cleveland in November to meet the boy as he lay in a hospital, gasping for air, his young lungs giving out on him. Among the gifts Journey brought with them was a cassette containing the band's upcoming single, an outtake from their 1983 hit album, *Frontiers*, soon to be released on the soundtrack to the film *Vision Quest.* That song was "Only the Young."

Kenny became one of the very first Journey fans to hear the song, as he played it on his Walkman while the band stood by his bedside. Eventually, the visit came to an end, and Journey returned to their homes in California. Their time with Kenny, however, deeply affected them, and the band would honor the boy on their 1986 tour by opening each concert with "Only the Young."

Being a huge Journey fan raised in Cleveland, I naturally read the story of this visit as it appeared in the Cleveland *Plain Dealer*. I was 14 at the time. Like most teenagers, I scanned the article in the newspaper looking for information that interested me most, coming away thinking that Journey was a cool band for traveling all that way to visit a sick boy and how cool it was that they'd brought a new song.

If I'd been more aware, I would have dug deeper. I would have realized that Kenny Sykaluk had a disease that could be linked to my own family. My cousin, also named Kenny and several years older than me, had a son just 5 years younger than me who passed away from CF when I was a boy. I didn't know him very well when we were growing up. The fact that we only saw my father's side of the family once a year made it difficult for me, at a young age, to feel a strong connection.

If I'd been more aware, I would've also followed up on the fate of Kenny Sykaluk. Sadly, he died soon after meeting his heroes. It is said that his Walkman was in his hand, the Journey tape still in it.

I remained a Journey fan throughout high school and into college, even when it wasn't cool and the band was considered derivative corporate dinosaurs. One of the reasons I continued to enjoy their music was the Kenny Sykaluk story. Despite the slick direction their music took at the end of the '80s and the in-fighting that led to the band's first breakup, the story made them seem less like rock stars and more like decent people capable of kindness.

Their actions in that October of 1984, like the lyrics and music of "Only the Young," gave me hope.

For Christmas in 1992, Julie bought me the Journey box set, *Time 3*. Besides the thrill of hearing several unreleased tracks from one of my favorite bands, I was excited to finally add "Only the Young" to my record collection. Because I'd owned all of Journey's studio albums, I never purchased their multi-platinum *Greatest Hits* album from 1988. I figured that I could make my own (bigger and better) "best of" compilation tape using my LP's and borrow the *Vision Quest* soundtrack from the library to add "Only the Young." Now that I had the song in a clean, digital form, it never sounded better.

The 63-page booklet in *Time 3* details the colorful history of Journey and includes the story of Journey's visit to Kenny Sykaluk. The booklet, of course, mentions CF, but I still didn't connect how that disease related to my own life. The story of Journey's Cleveland visit would be revisited in the late 1990s when Journey was featured on VH1's *Behind the Music*. In that hour long documentary, Steve Perry, Neal Schon and Jonathan Cain, the chief songwriters of Journey and the men responsible for "Only the Young," spoke about how meeting Kenny Sykaluk changed them and gave them a new perspective on life. Cain even broke into tears on camera.

You could be cynical and say that the Journey members were using this poor boy's death to be opportunistic in an attempt to make themselves look better. I don't believe that to be true. The way I see it, each time Journey and their fans mention Kenny Sykaluk and the horrible disease of cystic fibrosis, they not only keep his memory alive but also bring awareness to a little-known disease. They're doing their small part to help find a cure and stamp out CF once and for all.

I've seen Journey in concert three times, the last one being in August of 2001. I didn't know what to expect from the band, as they were touring in support of a new album and had a new lead singer, Steve Augeri. Would the music have the same power and the same emotion? Could Augeri's voice come close to the range and emotion of the legendary Steve Perry's? My worries were quelled when Journey began playing "Only the Young." Augeri hit each note perfectly and the band was flawless. What I've always loved about "Only the Young" is Neal Schon's understated guitar playing, how it complements the vocals and melody and doesn't overpower the rest of the band. On that hot summer night, Schon delivered each note with the same intensity and soulfulness that he did in 1986, when I heard them play the song the live for first time.

Jacob was born in November of 2001 and diagnosed with cystic fibrosis a month later. As Julie and I grappled with this news, distressed at what it meant to our baby boy's life, we leaned on our families and friends and turned to music to soothe our weary souls. Out of pure coincidence, Budd gave me *The Essential Journey* for my birthday in early November, so I had been listening to a lot of the group's classic songs. You've heard of comfort food? Well, Journey soon became comfort music.

It wasn't until the following spring, while re-reading the booklet from *Time 3*, that I finally connected the link between Journey's "Only the Young" and cystic fibrosis. So many years had passed and I had never once thought to look into the disease associated with one of my favorite songs by one of my favorite bands. Now that I was a father with a son afflicted with the same disease, the song took on a new meaning. I never listened to it the same way again. However, I never had a cathartic moment listening to it; I never felt a swell of emotions that caused me to associate the song with Jacob. It remained *that* song, linked to CF, but not a song about my family.

Until last weekend.

The city of Santa Clarita hosted a free concert in the park with the Journey tribute band DSB (Don't Stop Believin'). Julie, Sophie, Jacob and I joined 14,000 other people, old and young, to listen to a cover band perform the Journey hits. I have to say that the guys in DSB were top notch, putting on the closest thing to hearing Journey in concert besides the real deal. As they began their 18-song set of Journey classics (including several deep cuts), Sophie and I stood close to the stage to get the real concert experience. After about five songs, she'd had enough of her ears ringing, and we walked back to join Jacob and Julie, some 10,000 people back.

We sat in lawn chairs, ate Italian ice, watched the strange people walking around the park and enjoyed the music of Journey.

Midway through the set, DSB played "Only the Young." For the first time in my life, all of the elements about this song aligned. Journey, CF, and now my family. As the music soared, I looked at my precious son, then over to his darling sister and finally to my radiant wife. A huge wave of emotion swept over me. I have listened to this song at least a thousand times in 25 years, but it has never brought me to tears, not like it did that night, and not like it does as I'm writing this.

No longer would I associate the song with Journey's visit to a dying boy in 1984. The sadness that surrounded that day, which always seemed to be just below the surface of the song (for me), has been replaced with hope. I refuse to let this song make my heart hurt. I now have a lasting memory, one filled with smiling faces and the love of my family, to drive me. I will only let the optimism of "Only the Young" inspire me to do all that I can to ensure that CF is something my son lives with…but is not defined by.

When the song came to an end, I wiped my eyes and took a drag from the beer I was cradling. Soon thereafter, Julie and Jacob went home so that he could do his breathing treatments. By the end of the concert, Sophie and I returned to the front of the stage to hear DSB complete their triumphant show with a final round of hits, including Journey's signature anthem, "Don't Stop Believin'." No concert is complete without the band playing that one.

As far as I was concerned, it already was.

LINER NOTES

"The Rainbow Connection," by Kermit the Frog (Jim Henson), was written by Kenneth Ascher and Paul Williams. It appears on the 1979 soundtrack to the film *The Muppet Movie.*

"Rock Lobster," by The B-52's, was written by Kate Pierson, Fred Schneider, Keith Strickland, Cindy Wilson and Ricky Wilson. It appears on the band's 1979 debut album, *The B-52's.*

The Journey album *Escape* was released in 1981.

"Baba O'Riley," by The Who, was written by Pete Townshend. It appears on the band's 1971 album, *Who's Next.*

"Wrapped Around Your Finger," by The Police, was written by Sting. It appears on the band's 1983 album, *Synchronicity.*

"Kentucky Avenue," written and performed by Tom Waits, appears on his 1978 album, *Blue Valentine.*

"On the Turning Away," by Pink Floyd, was written by David Gilmour and Anthony Moore. It appears on the band's 1987 album, *A Momentary Lapse of Reason.*

"The Old Playground," by Bruce Hornsby & the Range, was written by Bruce Hornsby and John Hornsby. It appears on the band's 1988 album, *Scenes from the Southside.*

"Ana Ng," by They Might Be Giants, was written by John Flansburgh and John Linnell. It appears on the band's 1988 album, *Lincoln.*

"Rush," by Big Audio Dynamite, was written by Mick Jones. It appears on the band's 1991 album, *The Globe.*

"And So It Goes," written and performed by Billy Joel, appears on his 1989 album, *Storm Front.*

"Galileo," by Indigo Girls, was written by Emily Saliers. It appears on the duo's 1992 album, *Rites of Passage.*

"What About Now," by Robbie Robertson, was written by Robbie Robertson and Ivan Neville. It appears on Robertson's 1991 album, *Storyville.*

"Book of Dreams," written and performed by Bruce Springsteen, appears on his 1992 album, *Lucky Town.*

"Southern Accents," by Tom Petty & the Heartbreakers, was written by Tom Petty. It appears on the band's 1985 album, *Southern Accents.*

"Be Still," by Los Lobos, was written David K. Hidalgo and Louie F. Perez, Jr. It appears on the band's 1990 album, *The Neighborhood.*

"Distant Sun," by Crowded House, was written by Neil Finn. It appears on the band's 1994 album, *Together Alone.*

"Let's Stay Together," by Al Green, was written by Al Green, Willie Mitchell and Al Jackson, Jr. It appears on the Green's 1972 album, *Let's Stay Together.*

"Landslide," by Fleetwood Mac, was written by Stevie Nicks. The 1997 live version appears on the band's album *The Dance.*

"(Everything I Do) I Do It for You," by Bryan Adams, was written by Bryan Adams, Michael Kamen and Robert John "Mutt" Lange. It appears on the 1991 soundtrack to the film *Robin Hood: Prince of Thieves*, as well as Adams' 1991 album, *Waking Up the Neighbours.*

"Video Killed the Radio Star," by The Buggles, was written by Geoff Downes, Trevor Horn and Bruce Woolley. It appears on the band's 1980 album, *The Age of Plastic.*

"Here Comes the Sun," by The Beatles, was written by George Harrison. It appears on the band's 1969 album, *Abbey Road.*

Bruce Springsteen's album *The Rising* was released in 2002.

"Heavenly Day," written and performed by Patty Griffin, appears on her 2007 album, *Children Running Through.*

"Hard Sun," by Eddie Vedder, was written by Indio. It appears on Vedder's 2007 soundtrack to the film *Into the Wild.*

"Running to Stand Still," by U2, was written by Bono (lyrics) and U2 (music). It appears on the band's 1987 album, *The Joshua Tree.*

"For Good," was written by Stephen Schwartz. It appears on the 2003 original Broadway Cast Recording of the musical *Wicked.*

"One Cool Remove," by Shawn Colvin and Mary Chapin Carpenter, was written by Greg Brown. It appears on Colvin's 1994 album, *Cover Girl.*

"'Cross the Green Mountain," written and performed by Bob Dylan, appears on the 2003 soundtrack to the film *Gods and Generals.* It was later included on Dylan's 2008 compilation, *The Bootleg Series, Volume 8: Tell Tale Signs.*

"Only the Young," by Journey, was written by Jonathan Cain, Steve Perry and Neal Schon. It appears on the 1985 soundtrack to the film *Vision Quest.* It was later included on Journey's 1988 album, *Greatest Hits.*

"Trees," by Porcupine Tree, was written by Steven Wilson. It appears on the band's 2002 album, *In Absentia.*

ACKNOWLEDGEMENTS

I'd like to thank the following for their years of support and cajoling:

The staff of Popdose, home of Basement Songs, in particular Jon Cummings, Dw. Dunphy and Will Harris.

Special thanks to Jeff Giles, who has championed this column since its original inception.

The readers of Basement Songs, new and old. I used to joke that there were only ten of you. I know that to be so not true.

Dick Grunert and Jeff Marsick for editorial assistance.

The friends and relatives who've stood by me throughout the years.

Con amore, mio fratello, Stephen Keadey.

My family, especially Mom and Dad. It was in your basement that I fell in love with music and began my life as a writer.

Finally, I once again express my love to Julie, Sophie and Jacob for their unconditional love. Because of you, I am a better man.

ABOUT CYSTIC FIBROSIS

Cystic fibrosis is an inherited chronic disease that affects the lungs and digestive system of about 30,000 children and adults in the United States (70,000 worldwide). A defective gene and its protein product cause the body to produce unusually thick, sticky mucus that:

- Clogs the lungs and leads to life-threatening lung infections
- Obstructs the pancreas and stops natural enzymes from helping the body break down and absorb food

In the 1950s, few children with cystic fibrosis lived to attend elementary school. Today, advances in research and medical treatments have further enhanced and extended life for children and adults with CF. Many people with the disease can now expect to live into their 30s, 40s and beyond.

For more information on how you can help find a cure for cystic fibrosis, please visit www.cff.org

100% of the profits from the sale of *Basement Songs* will be donated to the Cystic Fibrosis Foundation.

BONUS TRACK

The genesis of this book dates back a couple of years to a night I spent dining with my Popdose colleagues, Jon Cummings and Will Harris. My two friends, both enthusiastic supporters of the column, urged me to compile my favorite Basement Songs into a book. Although I thought the idea was interesting, I dragged my feet for a long time. At the rate I was going, a Basement Songs book was never going to see the light of day.

Then, tragedy struck our family in December of 2011 when my brother-in-law, Seann Flynn, was killed in a traffic accident. Needless to say, our lives have never been the same since the phone calls we received that Monday afternoon. Among Seann's many talents, he was a gifted musician who wrote, recorded and released his own music independently. A true citizen of the digital age, Seann was proud of his art and wanted it heard. The Internet allowed him to achieve this. Inspired by Seann's fearlessness, I finally began working on this book.

What you've been reading wouldn't exist if it wasn't for my brother-in-law, plain and simple. I wish to God that it hadn't taken his passing to kick me in the ass and get it done. After Seann's death, I wrote the following Basement Songs column as a tribute to my fallen brother. As with the rest of the book, I hope that you enjoy it.

R.I.P. Seann Patrick Flynn
January 15, 1982 ~ December 5, 2011

PORCUPINE TREE
"TRAINS"

I could sense a presence at the foot of my bed; someone standing there, waiting for me to wake up. Raising my head, my eyes fought their way through the haze caused by the alcohol and turkey I'd consumed the night before. It was my brother-in-law, Seann, dressed in his motorcycle jacket and his backpack hanging over one shoulder. His mouth curled into the cocksure smile that never seemed to leave his face.

The night before, Thanksgiving, he'd joined us for a feast at my brother's house. We hadn't seen Seann in a while, and it was a pleasure to catch up. All in attendance came from Karyn's side of the family yet I always found it beautiful that Seann could effortlessly fit in with them. Just as they had welcomed Julie and me into their lives many years ago, they did the same with Seann. It helped that he was so personable and an interesting individual to be around. If you asked him, he could talk to you about just about anything.

It wasn't always that way, though. When I first met Seann, he was a cute, ten-year-old boy in love with the Cleveland Indians and the game of baseball. He was also pretty nonverbal. Our conversations generally went something like this:

Me: "What's up, dude?"

Seann: "Hmm. Not much."

Me: "Indians look pretty good. I really like the team they've put together, including that Lofton guy! I love him!"

Seann: "Hmm."

And that was about it. I was content with having this type of relationship with Seann seeing as I'd bonded with Julie's other brother, Michael, over shared interests in music, movies and comics. Still, I hoped that someday Seann and I might connect, despite the fact that Julie and I lived in California and he resided in Northeast Ohio.

Everything changed the day Seann took up drumming.

Having played drums throughout my entire adolescence and into college, I could finally relate to my young brother-in-law and really get to know him. To my great surprise, Seann didn't just bang around on the drums, playing to the radio; he excelled at the instrument through discipline, hours of practice and an innate sense of rhythm. He found a way to express himself, and it was awesome. As any drummer can tell you, it's a joy to listen and watch a natural talent on the kit, and Seann was a true natural. We now spoke the same language. Instead of grunts and mumbles, Seann and I began having conversations about drum kits, tuning, cymbal brands, drumsticks and which drummers he admired the most.

I'll admit that I took secret pleasure in being able to jam every time Julie and I went back to Cleveland, and Seann was always gracious to give up his drum stool whenever I asked. There were occasions when he would hang out just to watch me play. I'll wager to say, though, that he didn't receive as much pleasure in watching me as I did when he was behind his kit.

When the time came for Seann to apply to colleges, I was intrigued that he was considering Bowling Green State University, my alma mater. He wanted to major in music and seeing as I'd spent four years roaming the halls of BG's music school, I felt that I could offer my two cents. We discussed the school's excellent music program and the great campus atmosphere. I'm not sure if what I had to say had any sway in his decision, but Seann chose BG in the fall of 2000.

At Bowling Green, Sean transformed from a great drummer into well-rounded percussionist and musician. His studies introduced him to a variety of instruments that added richness to his skills. In addition, he became interested in sound engineering and began thinking about a career as a sound designer for films.

It was such a marvel to watch the light of his spirit shine. This was no truer than when he returned from a trip to Ghana, Africa. An openness and a joy for life were bursting from him as he regaled the family with stories of his trip abroad. Africa had fortified his soul and given him a new purpose in life.

In 2005, Seann graduated from college and moved to Los Angeles. In Southern California he really came into his own. For a short time he slept on our couch, made daily treks over the mountain into Hollywood and soon hooked up with some Ohio friends in that area, taking up residence on *their* couch. Eventually, he found a place in Venice, a city close to the beach and full of culture.

With the two industries in which he wanted to succeed surrounding him, Seann flourished. Moreover, the access to nature – oceans, forests, mountains – kept him in tune with his physical and spiritual sides. We began seeing less of him as his new life took off and he became busier, working as a sound designer and composer for a small production company, even recording and distributing his own music.

Still, Seann was never too busy to visit when we called. All it took was the pleading voice of Sophie on the other end of the phone and he would ride up to our house on his motorcycle for a home-cooked dinner and quality catching up. Each year when it came time for the CF Great Strides walks, he never had to be reminded. In fact, he would ask when the walk was taking place so that he could program it into his calendar. I will never forget his dedication to the children, not just to my kids, who had the good fortune of seeing him regularly, but also to his nieces and nephews who lived on the other side of the country.

Whenever the two of us got together, I was eager to talk about film, music or baseball. I never would have given Avenged Sevenfold a chance if it hadn't been off of his recommendation, I would not have been able to say that Thirty Seconds to Mars is not my thing, and I never would have discovered Porcupine Tree, the British prog metal band with a cult following in America.

During the Christmas of 2010, as I scrolled through his iTunes, their album, *In Absentia*, popped up on the screen.

"Those guys are great," he told me, "you really should listen to them."

Intrigued, I copied the album to my iPod. Months later, while commuting to work, I fell in love with the record. The multiple time changes, the lush harmonies, the slick production – everything reminded me of my favorite Yes album from 1983, *90125*. In particular, the second track, "Trains," stuck its hooks into me and had me singing it for days. Because he was the only person I knew who'd ever heard of this band, I always associated the album with Seann.

It should come as no surprise that when Seann was killed in a traffic accident last December, I sought comfort in the music that made me feel closest to him. To numb the hours, days and weeks following his tragic death, to block out the screaming in my head and the hot tears of sorrow, I listened to "Trains" over and over again – on the train, in my office and before I went to bed, forcing myself to sleep. Sometimes it was a great help, and at others it was just the noise I needed to help me get through the grieving.

I'm so fortunate to have known this man. As I said, he was a good uncle, a good friend and a brother to me. Was Seann perfect? No. But who in their 20's is? He was still learning, growing, trying to figure out this world and how to make it better, trying to find his place in it. I'm so glad that he decided to spend Thanksgiving with us last year, to have him join us in the good food and company that the holiday symbolizes. The next morning, while Jacob slept and Julie was out shopping with Sophie, Seann entered my bedroom to say goodbye before leaving.

It was the last time I ever saw him.

He stood at the end of my bed, dressed in his motorcycle jacket, his backpack hanging over one shoulder. His mouth curled into the cocksure smile that never seemed to leave his face. I craned my neck to look at him.

"S'up?" I asked.

"I'm taking off," he replied.

"Mmm, yeah."

"Tell Julie I said goodbye."

"Hmm. Yeah. Sure."

"See ya."

"See ya."

I fell back on to my pillow while Seann left the house.

He walked across the driveway and started up his motorcycle, parked right outside the bedroom window.

As I drifted back to sleep, I could hear the sound of his motorcycle drive down our street and fade off into the distance.

N.R YES NO
FROM SCOTT, AUG. '92
R 90
B
maxell
POSITION NORMAL

www.ingramcontent.com/pod-product-compliance
Lightning Source LLC
LaVergne TN
LVHW050633100826
845148LV00011B/1850

* 9 7 8 0 5 7 8 1 1 5 5 1 1 *